GANDHIAN HUMANISM

GANDHIAN STUDIES AND PEACE RESEARCH SERIES

1. **Gandhian Model of Development and World Peace**/ R.P. Misra
2. **Conflict Resolution Through Non-Violence:** Role of the Universities/ K.D. Gangrade & R.P. Misra (**Volumen 1: Science and Ethics**)
3. **Conflict Resolution Through Non-Violence:** Role of the Universities/ K.D. Gangrade & R.P. Misra (**Volume 2: Development Without Destruction**)
4. **Social Philosophy of Mahatma Gandhi (The)**/ K.S. Bharathi
5. **Gandhian Humanism**/ Mohit Chakrabarti
6. **Gandhian Holistic Economics**/ Shashi Prabha Sharma
7. **Gandhian Spiritualism**/ Mohit Chakrabarti
8. **Gandhian Perspective on Population and Development**/ A.K. Sharma
9. **Thoughts of Gandhi and Vinoba:** A Comparative Study/ K.S. Bharathi
10. **Economic Philosophy of Mahatma Gandhi**/ Shanti Swarup Gupta
11. **Encyclopaedia of Eminent Thinkers (Volume 1 : The Political Thought of Mahatma Gandhi)**/ K.S. Bharathi
12. **Gandhi and 21st Century**/ Janardan Pandey (Ed.)
13. **Gandhian Philosophy of the Spinning Wheel (The)**/ Mohit Chakrabarti
14. **Gandhian Satyagraha**/ Ajay Shanker Rai
15. **Gandhi and His Religion**/ Dr. (Lt.Col.) P.A. Raju
16. **महात्मा गाँधी विचार-वीथिका/** सुरेन्द्र प्रसाद अग्रवाल
17. **Poverty of Gandhian Philosophy**/ Himansu Roy
18. **Right to Equality in The Indian Constitution**/ Shashi Nath Saraswati
19. **Meditations on Gandhi**/ M.P. Mathai, M.S. John and S.K. Joseph (Eds.)
20. **Politico-Economic Ideas of Mahatma Gandhi**/ Sukhendu Mazumder
21. **Moral Lessons from Gandhi's Autobiography and Other Essays**/ K.D. Gangrade
22. **Fire Sans IRE:** A Critical Study of Gandhian Non-Violence/ Mohit Chakrabarti
23. **Gandhian Alternative (Volume 1 : Towards a Gandhian World Order)** Suresh Misra (Ed.)
24. **Gandhian Alternative (Volume 2 : Nonviolence in Action)**/ Savita Singh and Bharati Misra (Eds.)
25. **Gandhian Alternative (Volume 3 : Socio-Political Thoughts)**/ Anil Dutta Mishra and Sushma Yadav (Eds.)
26. **Gandhian Alternative (Volume 4 : Economics Where People Matter)**/ V.K. Natraj, Kamlesh Misra and Neeru Kapoor (Eds.)
27. **Gandhian Alternative (Volume 5 : Education for Human Development)**/ Suresh Misra (Ed.)
28. **Gandhian Approach to Development Planning**/ Ram Binod Singh

GANDHIAN STUDIES AND PEACE RESEARCH SERIES-5

GANDHIAN HUMANISM

Mohit Chakrabarti

CONCEPT PUBLISHING COMPANY PVT. LTD.
NEW DELHI-110059

ISBN-13: 978-81-7022-383-2

First Published 1992

Published and Printed by

Concept Since 1974

Concept Publishing Company Pvt. Ltd.
A/15-16, Commercial Block, Mohan Garden
New Delhi-110059 (India)
T: 25351460, 25351794, *F*: 091-11-25357109
E: publishing@conceptpub.com, W: www.conceptpub.com
Editorial Office: H-13, Bali Nagar, New Delhi-110 015, India.

Cataloging in Publication Data--Courtesy: D.K. Agencies (P) Ltd. <docinfo@dkagencies.com>

Chakrabarti, Mohit, 1941- **author.**
Gandhian humanism / Mohit Chakrabarti.
pages cm. -- (Gandhian studies and peace research series ; 5)
Includes bibliographical references and index.
ISBN 9788170223832

1. Gandhi, Mahatma, 1869-1948--Philosophy. 2. Humanism--History--20th century. I. Title. II. Series: Gandhian studies and peace research series ; 5.

DS481.G3C43 2016 DDC 954.035 23

Dedicated to

Swami Mumukshananda
Shri Ramakrishna Ashrama
RAJKOT 360001

to whom my debts
are endless

PREFACE

If HUMANISM is man's real identity as man, Gandhian humanism is more than that. He goes deeper into the problems of human consciousness and probes into the inner sensibilities of mankind. There are neither any theories nor are there any dogmas to uphold humanism as something novel or new in him but where he departs from others in evolving a new concept of humanism is : it is Love and Truth for which man is and eternally thrives for the fusion of man and the All Beautiful. "Gandhian Humanism : Inroads to Inner Awakening" and "Objectives and Strategies of Gandhian Humanism" are pointers to the essence of Gandhian Humanism.

That religion is nothing but to synchronise diverse faiths and religious beliefs towards the welfare of mankind is discussed in "Religion and Humanism : Gandhian Guidelines". What makes Gandhi rather a revolutionary is that the socio-cultural aspects of humanism find a new language in his service towards humanity — a fact discussed in "Socio-cultural Aspects of Gandhian Humanism".

The Gandhian aesthetics of *Sarvodaya* is undoubtedly a new dimension in the discovery of human consciousness. It is a concept that embraces humanity for global awareness and global welfare. "*Sarvodaya* and Gandhian Humanism" is an introspective analysis to this end in view.

Education is always looking within and looking in askance for the exploration of inner consciousness. It is a means to find out and utilise the natural and available resources towards the well-being of mankind. Gandhi, therefore, looks upon education as an unending preparation for service towards mankind in course of self-askance, self-discovery, self-enrichment and self-evolution. "The Humanistic Approach to Education : Gandhian Viewpoints" is a critical study on these viewpoints of education.

"Gandhian Humanism and Non-violence" and "Tagore and Gandhi : Harbingers of Humanism" earnestly expect learned criticism from esteemed readers.

My debts to Srimat Swami Mumukshanandaji Maharaj, President,

Shri Ramakrishna Ashrama, Rajkot-360001, India are boundless. I humbly dedicate my book to him as a token of reverence.

One Luminous, Creator of All, Mahatma, Gandhi is a great ocean of humanism. To be recognised as a little drop in that ocean is more than a reward for a tyro like me. The rest awaits the response of revered readers.

Seemantika
Visva-Bharati University — MOHIT CHAKRABARTI
Santiniketan-731235
West Bengal, India

CONTENTS

Preface 7

1. Gandhian Humanism : Inroads to Inner Awakening 11
2. Objectives and Strategies of Gandhian Humanism 25
3. Religion and Humanism : Gandhian Guidelines 42
4. The Socio-cultural Aspects of Gandhian Humanism 59
5. Sarvodaya and Gandhian Humanism 80
6. Non-violence and Gandhian Humanism 106
7. The Humanistic Approach to Education : Gandhian Viewpoints 137
8. Tagore and Gandhi : Harbingers of Humanism 160

Index 176

1

GANDHIAN HUMANISM : Inroads to Inner Awakening

THE BIRTH of man is a mystery as well as a muse. It is a mystery because it is born in the womb of beyondings. It is a muse because it sings the glory of the All Beautiful. As a mysterious being, man haunts within, and also outside himself, for the unknown and unseen, unlearnt and unfelt, unendeared and unappreciated. As a man of muse, he plays on in the lyre of his mind the muse of the Great Master who is also the Eternal Singer of the goodness of mankind.

Is man aware of the mysterious nature of himself? Is he conscious of the muse within ? Is there a real synthesis between mystery and muse within himself ? What are the patterns of exposures of mystery and muse under diverse circumstances ? What are the manifold dimensions of his thoughts and feelings, reasonings and appreciations consequential to his experiences right from the moment of his birth till his death ? A host of such other askances brings forth unending dimensions to human evolution.

Side-by-side with these diverse avenues of human evolution, man today is at the crossroad of an unavoidable ukase: Flourish or perish. Human imagination is ruthlessly toyed with automation, super-computerisation, Mega-machines and what not. A computerised society is sacked within the limits of computerised imagination. A robotised society with its ceremonial parade of software makes a macabre moratorium of humanism. The lot of the bewailing humanity awaits a further doom.

Perhaps the waning of the setting sun heralds the glory of the dazzling dawn of tomorrow. The agonies of today are the bright green signals of the day that follows. Is man a phoenix of purity of thoughts and perfection of promises ?

An apostle of humanism, Gandhi shows inroads to inner awakening. For him, the discovery of the man within man is the starting point of humanism. It is, as he deeply believes, a means to an end and never an end in itself. For he also believes in the beyonding of man. Therefore, whatever avenues of excellence are discovered by man through humanistic endeavour are mere entry-points for beyonding. The real urge for humanism will ignite man in stick-to-itiveness to work alone and not the outcome of work to seek in vain for an end or result. The underlying principle is that one has the authority to work and work only and should never expect for work that yields fruit:

Karmanyevadhikaraste tu ma phalesu kadachana

— *Srimad Bhagavad Gita*, Chapter II

An ardent follower of the above principle of work, Gandhi maintains strict adherence to duty as a part of humanistic enterprise. Quite realistically, he elucidates his principle of work as a part of humanism in his own unique fashion:

> True to his poetical instinct, the poet lives for the morrow and would have us do likewise. He presents to our admiring gaze the beautiful picture of the birds early in the morning singing hymns of praise as they soar into the sky. These birds have had their day's food and soared with rested wings, in whose veins new blood had flown during the previous night. But I have had the pain of watching birds who for want of strength could not be coaxed even into a flutter of their wings. The human bird under the Indian sky gets up weaker than when he pretended to retire. For millions it is an eternal vigil or an eternal trance. It is an indescribably painful state which has got to be experienced to be realised. I have found it impossible to soothe suffering patients with a song from Kabir. The hungry millions ask for one poem — invigorating food. They cannot be given it. They must earn it. And they can earn only by the sweat of their brow.

— Mahatma Gandhi : *Young India*, 13 October, 1921, p. 326.

Probing psychologically into the weakness of the 'human bird' as Gandhi poetically does with symbolic interpretations, he also rejects dependence or spoonfeeding of humanity drastically and inspires for 'invigorating food' as the primary poem of humanism. The real awakening of humanism as he rightly feels, is self-activity and self-dependence that allow every man to be worthy of his existence. To be attuned with the spirit of work for oneself and for everyone is to be prepared for the worship of humanity which is, as Gandhi ardently believes, the worship of God.

Quite realistically, Gandhi advocates for humanism in the strict discipline of honouring oneself by doing justice to the 'man' in oneself. This is further revealed in one's consciousness for self-dependence and self-honour. The idea of self-respect will automatically thrive in oneself only when one is continually alert in performing one's duties and responsibilities to the best of one's abilities. It is, therefore, a shame to remain idle and depend on others for bare existence. It belittles oneself and humanity, too. A sense of humiliation to humanity consequential to passivity and neglect of self-activity crushes the very foundation of human civilisation. The introduction of *Charkha* or the spinning wheel points towards the revival of the inner consciousness of humanity. Gandhi categorically elucidates this philosophy of work as a humanistic enterprise :

> Do not say you will maintain the poor on charity. Only two classes of people are entitled to charity and no one else — the *Brahmana* who possesses nothing and whose business it is to spread holy learning, and the cripple and the blind. The iniquitous system of giving doles to the able-bodied idle is going on to our eternal shame and humiliation, and it is to wipe out that shame that I am going about with the message of the *Charkha* up and down the whole country.
>
> — M. K. Gandhi : *Young India*, February 24, 1927, p. 58.

A certain sense of stick-to-itiveness to work which is as Gandhi ardently believes, at the root of humanism should be the basis of our education. The education of *Swaraj* is, indeed, the education of the spinning wheel that teaches that true spirit of inner consciousness exercised in all humility and sincerity. Gandhi's own interpretation clarifies the point better :

> All natural and necessary work is easy. Only it requires

> constant practice to become perfect, and it needs plodding. Ability to plod is *Swaraj*. It is *yoga*. Nor need the reader be frightened of the monotony. Monotony is the law of nature. Look at the monotonous manner in which the sun rises. And imagine the catastrophe that would befall the universe if the sun become capricious and went in for a variety of pastime. But there is a monotony that sustains and monotony that kills. The monotony of necessary occupations is exhilarating and life-giving. An artist never tires of his art. A spinner who has mastered the art, will certainly be able to do sustained work without fatigue. There is a music about the spindle which the practised spinner catches without fail. And when India has monotonously worked away at turning out *Swaraj*, she will have produced a thing of beauty which will be a joy forever. But it cannot be without the spinning wheel. Therefore, the best national education for India is undoubtedly an intelligent handling of the spinning wheel.
>
> — M. K. Gandhi : *Young India*, 18 August 1921, p. 262.

The education of awareness by means of the spinning wheel as designed by Mahatma Gandhi in his practical approach to *Nayee Talim* or Basic Education is the key to Gandhian humanism. To be aware of oneself is to nursle the seedlings of the good sense and sensibilities within oneself. Gandhi emphasises on the humanistic approach to education rather than mere accomplishments in scholastic endeavour. While giving a reply to the warm words of appreciation made by the leading members like Professor Davies, Professor Bovet and Dr. Zilliacus of the New Education Fellowship programme, who were the guests and who widely and thoroughly studied the Gandhian concept of Basic Education as a very viable humanistic approach to education, Gandhi adroitly remarks :

> I am greatful that so many educationists have blessed the new scheme. There have been critics also; but when I launched the scheme I did not know that it would appeal to anyone beyond the circle of my co-workers. When I consider the masses of India and the masses situated as they are, I could not think of any other type of education. With them work must precede anything else, and the concern of an educationist is to make

> that work educative. Let every child feel that he creates something for use and also expands his mind and heart therethrough.
>
> — M. K. Gandhi : Address to the members of the New Education Fellowship Programme. Quoted from *Mahatma* by D.G. Tendulkar, Publications Division, Ministry of Information and Broadcasting. Government of India, Vol. IV, p. 200.

Undeniably, the education of expansion of the mind and the heart is the only education that fosters humanism and the true spirit of humanism thrives only when there is a continual cultivation of the spirit of total human welfare. To make a child prepared for that type of education—useful, purposeful, meaningful, life-centric and humanistic—is to march ahead with the spirit of human progress, peace and prosperity.

Moreover, the philosophy of education received through spinning by a learner in course of undergoing Basic Education programmes ensures the fact that the true purpose of education is to receive the education of the total man. So any attempt at imparting education cannot but introduce activities that incorporate the philosophy of total manhood in education. Gandhi elucidates this concept of the development of 'the full man' very characteristically :

> My idea is not merely to teach a particular profession or occupation to the children, but to develop the full man through teaching that occupation. He will not only learn weaving, for instance, but learn why be should weave in a particular fashion and not any other, why he should handle yearn in a particular fashion and no other, and why he should himself know spinning and why should insist on a particular count for a particular kind of weaving. All these things the weaver boy does not learn at home. The spinning wheel is to him just what it was a thousand years ago. We make him learn the art of making the most efficient wheel and a loom, not so as to displace other labour but so as to make them more efficient than the existing models. . . . I want to bring about equalisation of status. The working classes have all these centuries been isolated and relegated to a lower status. They

> have been *Shudras*, and the word has been interpreted to mean an inferior status. I want to allow no differentiation between the son of a weaver, of an agriculturist and of a school master.
>
> — D. G. Tendulkar : *Mahatma*, Publications Division, Ministry of Information and Broadcasting, Government of India, Vol. IV, p. 201.

The principle of equality in the worth of man as man as one of the fundamental aspects of humanism has been highlighted by Gandhi not because he wants to streamline every activity in terms of performance but essentially because he primarily wants to bring about a certain sense of inner awakening in mankind. As a true humanist, he does not think a better alternative than the spinning wheel that alone can bring about a change in the sad lot of humanity.

In this connection one might recall Gandhi's own observations on the introduction of the spinning wheel, which he made in *Young India* in 1921:

> The only question therefore that a lover of India and humanity has to address himself to is how best to devise practical means of alleviating India's wretchedness and misery. No scheme of irrigation or other agricultural improvement that human ingenuity can conceive can deal with the vastly scattered population of India or provide work for masses of mankind who are constantly thrown out of employment. Imagine a nation working only five hours a day on an average, and this not by choice but by force of circumstances, and you have a realistic picture of India.
>
> — M. K. Gandhi : *Young India*, November 3, 1921, p. 350.

To bring about a change of the sad lot of millions of people sitting idly and facing economic stringency is what Gandhi considers to be of primary importance. As a humanist, he rightly signifies the point that self-dependence and not charity accelerates true humanism. In 1927, when the British rulers in India virtually made the people rather interested in depending on them for bare livelihood, Gandhi uncompromisingly steered a crusade against this British yoke by emphasising on the spinning wheel as the only alternative to save the yoked humanity. As he remarks,

> . . . I cannot be satisfied, not till every man and woman in India is working at his or at her wheel. Burn that wheel if you find a better substitute. This is the one and only work which can supply the needs of the millions without disturbing them from their homes.
>
> After all, a lip-profession of faith in the *Charkha* and the throwing of a few rupees at me in a patronising manner won't bring Swaraj and won't solve the problem of the ever-deepening poverty of the toiling and starving millions. I want to correct myself. I have said toiling millions. I wish that it was a true description. Unfortunately, as we have not revised our tastes about clothing, we have made it impossible for these starving millions to toil throughout the year. We have imposed upon them a vacation, which they do not need, for at least four months in the year. This is not a figment of my imagination, but it is a truth repeated by many English administrators, if you reject the testimony of your own countrymen who have moved in the midst of these masses. So then if I take this purse away and distribute it amongst the starving sisters, it does not solve the question. On the contrary, it will impoverish their soul. They will become beggars and get into the habit of living upon charity. Heaven help the man, the woman or the nation that learns to live on charity.
>
> — M. K. Gandhi : *Young India*, September 15, 1927, p. 313.

Notwithstanding the above observation on the role of the spinning wheel as the armour of self-dependence, Gandhi also considers the *Charkha* as the symbol of peace and prosperity, of goodwill and self-help. A strong sense of stick-to-itiveness to the spinning wheel would certainly bring forth worthy dividends in the forms of self-respect and freedom as desirable concepts of humanism. As Gandhi clarifies,

> The *Charkha* is a useful and indispensable article for every home. It is the symbol of the nation's prosperity and therefore freedom. It is a symbol not of commercial war but of

> commercial peace. It bears not a message of ill-will towards the nations of the earth but of goodwill and self-help. It will not need a navy threatening a world's peace and exploiting its resources; but it needs the religious determination of millions to spin their yarn in their own homes as today they cook their food in their own homes.
>
> — M. K. Gandhi : *Young India*, December 8, 1921, p. 406.

For the destiny of mankind to be moulded in the mirth of manhood, Gandhian humanism reorients man from the standpoint of truth and non-violence. While truth makes inroads to the essence of humanism, man as the agent of truth, seeks transcendence. Gandhian humanism builds the avenues of beyonding through strict adherence to non-violence. But the pattern of truth expressed or nursled and that of non-violence observed or carried out symbolises the incessant urge to be more purified in action and contemplation. As Gandhi poignantly observes,

> Truth and non-violence are perhaps the activist forces you have in the world. A man who wields sanguinary weapons and is intent upon destroying those whom he considers his enemies, does at least require some rest and has to lay down his arms for a while in every twenty-four hours. He is, therefore, essentially inactive for a certain part of the day. Not so the votary of truth and non-violence, for the simple reason that they are not external weapons. They reside in the human breast and they are actively working their way whether you are awake or asleep, whether you are walking leisurely or playing an active game. The panoplied warrior of truth and non-violence is ever and incessantly active.
>
> — D. G. Tendulkar : *Mahatma*, Publications Division, Ministry of Information and Broadcasting, Government of India, Vol. III, p. 145.

To be forearmed with the spirit of truth and non-violence is to be forewarned against demoralised humanity. Gandhi's own experiments with truth and non-violence point to this fact very significantly :

> To see the universal and all-pervading Spirit of Truth face to face one must be able to love the meanest of creation as oneself. And a man who aspires after that cannot afford to keep out of any field of life. That is why my devotion to Truth has drawn me into the field of politics; and I can say without the slightest hesitation, and yet in all humility, that those who say that religion has nothing to do with politics do not know what religion means.
>
> — M. K. Gandhi : *An Autobiography*, Navajivan Publishing House, Ahmedabad — 14. 1959, p. 370-371.

To consider Truth as part and parcel of religion is to heighten humanity towards nobler directions of realising and identifying with the wills of God. Gandhi, therefore, emphasises on self-purification as one of the fundamental ends in view of non-violence as a great humanistic force to reach 'the farthest limit of humility'. In the poignant words of Gandhi,

> Identification with everything that lives is impossible without self-purification; without self-purification the observance of the law of *Ahimsa* must remain an empty dream; God can never be realised by one who is not pure of heart. Self-purification therefore must mean purification in all the walks of life. And purification being highly infectious, purification of oneself necessarily leads to the purification of one's surroundings.
>
> But the path of self-purification is hard and steep. To attain to perfect purity one has to become absolutely passion-free in thought, speech and action; to rise above the opposing currents of love and hatred, attachment and repulsion. I know that I have not in me as yet that triple purity, in spite of constant ceaseless striving for it. That is why the world's praise fails to move me, indeed it very often stings me. To conquer the subtle passions seems to me to be harder far than the physical conquest of the world by the force of arms. Ever since my return to India I have had experiences of the dormant passions lying hidden within me. The knowledge of them has made me feel humiliated though not defeated. The experiences and experiments have sustained me

> and given me great joy. But I know that I have still before me a difficult path to traverse. I must reduce myself to zero. So long as a man does not of his own free will put himself last among his fellow creatures, there is no salvation for him. Ahimsa is the farthest limit of humility.
>
> —*Ibid*, p. 371.

The source point of humanism as Gandhi points out is to strive for perfection. He, therefore, makes no distinction between perfection and self-realisation that can only be attained through strict adherence to non-violence. Promotion of life and love as he rightly observes, paves avenues towards self-realisation better. It alone lifts mankind from pettiness of mind and selfishness in attitude — the two ugliest forces that drastically bring a sad end to humanism. It even blocks and bars all endeavour of good sense and sensibilities that act as inroads to awakening of humanism. Gandhi highlights purity of mind by means of exercise and observance of love and devotion to non-violence that does not, under any circumstances, compromise with any evil whatsoever. As he observes,

> Life is an aspiration. Its mission is to strive after perfection, which is self-realisation. The ideals must not be lowered because of our weaknesses and imperfections. . . . One who hooks his fortunes to *ahimsa*, the law of love, daily lessens the circle of destruction, and to that extent promotes life and love; he who swears by *himsa*, the law of hate, daily widens the circle of destruction, and to that extent promotes death and hate.
>
> — Pyarelal : *Mahatma Gandhi : The Last Phase* Navajivan Publishing House, Ahmedabad, Vol II, p. 507.

The law of love, and not the law of hate, as Gandhi proves in his action and contemplation dignifies humanism. It is this law of love, again, that shows mankind the right approach to manhood. As soon as man develops a sense of doing good to humanity, he enters into a new wonderland of sensibilities. Every bit of good sense within him is enkindled with a new aura of brilliance. Every bit of good sense eliminates animality. The curse of being man with every aspect of animality will by virtue of goodness be replaced and reduced to a cipher. Man, the great astronaut of consciousness, discovers and rediscovers himself by being a practical humanist.

An eternal symbol of practical humanism, Gandhi shows us the avenues of self-realisation and self-discovery in his autobiographical vein :

> My soul refuses to be satisfied so long as it is a helpless witness of a single wrong or a single misery. But it is not possible for me, a weak, frail, miserable being, to mend every wrong or to hold myself free of blame for all the wrong I see. The spirit in me pulls one way, the flesh in me pulls in the opposite direction. There is freedom from the action of these two forces but that freedom is attainable only by slow and painful stages. I cannot attain freedom by a mechanical refusal to act, but only by intelligent action in a detached manner. This struggle resolves itself into an incessant crucifixion of the flesh so that the spirit may become entirely free.
>
> — Pyarelal : *Mahatma Gandhi : The Last Phase,* Navajivan Publishing House, Ahmedabad Vol. II, p. 234.

The 'crucifixion of the flesh' by means of enrichment of the inner spirit of man is the Gandhian slogan of humanism that can only bring about a change of consciousness. A change for a negation of physical avarice and attachment through striving for perfection in the enriched pattern of life is what true humanism stands for. A little but cautious care of the littleness of oneself as he observes, saves one from being lost in the labyrinth of vainglory :

> Truth to me is infinitely dearer than the 'mahatmaship', which is purely a burden. It is my knowledge of my limitations and my nothingness which has so far saved me from the oppressiveness of 'mahatmaship'. I am painfully aware of the fact that my desire to continue life in the body involves me in constant *himsa,* that is why I am becoming growingly indifferent to this physical body of mine. For instance, I know that in the act of respiration I destroy innumerable invisible germs floating in the air. But I do not stop breathing. The

> consumption of vegetables involves *himsa* but I cannot give them up. Again, there is *himsa* in the use of antiseptic yet I cannot bring myself to discard the use of disinfectants like the kerosene, to rid myself of the mosquito pest and the like. I suffer snakes to be killed in the *ashram* when it is impossible to catch and put them out of harm's way. I even tolerate the use of the stick to drive the bullocks in the *ashram*. Thus there is no end of *himsa*, which I directly and indirectly commit. And now I find myself confronted with this monkey problem. Let me assure the reader that I am in no hurry to take the extreme step of killing them. In fact, I am not sure that I would at all be able finally to make up my mind to kill them. But I cannot promise that I shall never kill the monkeys even though they may destroy all the crops in the *ashram*. If as a result of this confession of mine, friends choose to give me up as lost I would be sorry, but nothing will induce me to try to conceal my imperfections in the practice of *ahimsa*. All I claim for myself is that I am ceaselessly trying to understand the implications of great ideals like *ahimsa* and practise them in thought, word and deed and that not without a certain measure of success, as I think. But I know that I have a long distance yet to cover in this direction.
>
> — D. G. Tendulkar : *Mahatma*, Publications Division, Ministry of Information and Broadcasting, Government of India, Vol. II, pp. 425-426.

For the unending march for attainment of perfection in life, Gandhi considers man as the symbol of untiring devotion to Truth and non-violence. Therefore, until and unless he purifies himself to such an extent as to contribute worthily towards the cause of better and greater human welfare, he cannot be truly humanistic. The inroads of humanism are to be identified in accordance with the approach to life towards perfection. A certain pattern of uniformity in thoughts, words and deeds towards humanistic endeavour is of utmost importance in leading a life for attainment of perfection and for these distillation of behavioural manifestations from ethical as well as aesthetic points of view takes a very prominent role. In fact, the true religion of man is the religion of humanism — the perfection of one and all through persistent endeavour in search of truth and goodness of mankind. That every individual heightens and glorifies himself by means of devotion and steadfastness to Truth and non-violence is the most significant point of Gandhian humanism.

Man, the best creature of the All Beautiful, proves his excellence by being human in his approach to God. The All Beautiful merges in him only when he feels and acts with the spirit of unison already in him. The divinity in man, as Gandhi proves in action, is in his interaction between the good and the evil, the right and the wrong, the light and the darkness within him. The appropriate avenues for human perfection are legion. It is the ardent duty of every man to harbour his good sense and sensibilities in this island of the All Beautiful within himself. This, then, will be the stepping stone to realisation of humanism, the true realisation of God. This then, will also be a prelude to the greetings for man, an inseparable and unified embodiment of God. As Gandhi remarks,

> Man's ultimate aim is the realisation of God, and all his activities, social, political, religious, have to be guided by the ultimate aim of the vision of God. The immediate service of all human beings becomes a necessary part of the endeavour, simply because the only way to find God is to see Him in His creation and be one with it. This can only be done by service of all. I am a part and parcel of the whole, and I cannot find Him apart from the rest of humanity. My countrymen are my nearest neighbours. They have become so helpless, so resourceless, so inert that I must concentrate myself on serving them. If I could persuade that I should find Him in a Himalayan cave I would proceed there immediately. But I know that I cannot find Him apart from Humanity.
>
> — M. K. Gandhi : *Harijan*, August 29, 1931, p. 226.

To consider countrymen 'nearest neighbours' is the essence of Gandhian humanism. It is the essence that characterises his ardent love for the God in man, the true God of humanism. It is this God, again, that allows him no rest to think and act for continual welfare of humanity. Apart from the fact that a certain sense of dedication for humanity makes life meaningful, the continual endeavour for awakening of the divinity in man points towards true humanism. This, if translated into reality, becomes a creed for the service of God, the

Daridranarayan, God embodied in the poor as Gandhi visualises.

What, then, should be the song of humanism? In the eternal words of prayer it transcends in Tagorean serenity:

> This is my prayer to thee, my lord —
> Strike, strike at the root of penury in my heart.
>
> Give me the strength lightly to bear my joys and sorrows.
>
> Give me the strength to make my love fruitful in service.
>
> Give me the strength never to disown the poor or bend my knees before insolent might.
>
> Give me the strength to raise my mind high above daily trifles.
>
> And give me the strength to surrender my strength to thy will with love.
>
> — Rabindranath Tagore : *Gitanjali*, Macmillan Pocket Tagore Edition, Macmillan India Limited. 1983 No. XXXVI, p. 21.

Who else than Gandhi can be a greater and worthier singer of the above song of humanism ?

2

OBJECTIVES AND STRATEGIES OF GANDHIAN HUMANISM

THE DESTINY of man rests on himself. It is he, and he alone, who moulds or mars his destiny. It is he who advances or retards within himself in accordance with his accomplishments. If he fails to utilise the potentialities within himself, the consequences are inevitably miserable. If, on the other hand, he continually strives for enrichment of himself, he better proves his worth. The essence of Gandhian humanism incorporates the eternal will of mankind towards awakening of the inner potentialities, towards awakening of the inner man. It is the inner man that marks the victory of man.

How does Gandhi find out the essence of excellence that marks the victory of man ? What are the objectives of the humanism he identifies? What strategies are to adopted for exercise of humanistic ideas and ideals, and how ? These are some of the questions that also call forth elucidation for better exposures of Gandhian mysticism.

As a matter of fact, the obscure ideas often nursled in sentimentalism and passivity encompassing the objectives and strategies of Gandhian humanism have more often damaged truth and endeared myth than explored the true vision of Gandhi as a humanist. Moreover, the crushed picture of a humanistic society under unforeseen and undesired circumstances for which the great visionary has nothing to do, makes more muddle in the concept of humanism. The truth lost is never the lost truth. Gandhian humanism is never a partner to sham humanism.

One of the fundamental objectives of Gandhian humanism is to be empowered with the weapon of self-restraint. This will enable an individual to guard himself against disrupting forces. It is an inner force that quickens his judgement to take action against all ills and evils however undesirable and unexpected.

Now, can an individual identify that the power of self-restraint is working within himself ? The answer, according to Gandhi, is very clear, and the strategies to be followed are inherent and spontaneous. As he observes,

> It is true that he who has attained perfect *brahmacharya* does not stand in need of protecting walls. But the aspirant undoubtedly needs them, even as a young mango plant has need of a strong fence round it. A child goes from its mother's lap to the cradle and from cradle to the pushcart — till he becomes a man who has learnt to walk without aid. To cling to the aid when it is needless is surely harmful.
>
> It appears to me that even the true aspirant does not need the above-mentioned restraints. *Brahmacharya* is not a virtue that can be cultivated by outward restraints. He who runs away from a necessary contact with a woman does not understand the full meaning of *brahmacharya*. However attractive a woman may be, her attraction will produce no effect on the man without the urge.
>
> The true *brahmachari* will shun false restraints. He must create his own fences according to his limitations, breaking them down when he feels that they are unnecessary. The first thing is to know what true *brahmacharya* is, then to realise its value, and lastly to try to cultivate this priceless virtue. I hold that true service of the country demands this observance.
>
> — Pyarelal : *Mahatma Gandhi : The Last Phase*, Navajivan Publishing House, Ahmedabad, Vol I, p. 600.

The above strategy of self-restraint in the form of a *brahmachari* as one of the Gandhian strategies of humane consciousness also encompasses another important objective of humanism. It is to practise in the control of sensualism, of temptation and sentimentalism. The important factors associated with this practice is to have a careful and cautious control over sense-organs. From *The Diary of Mahadev Desai,* we come across a better exposure of this Gandhian strategy of humanism in the observance of *brahmacharya* :

> Brahmacharya is such only if it persists under all conditions and in the face of every possible temptation. If a beautiful woman approaches the marble statue of a man it will not be

affected in the least. A *brahmachari* is one who reacts in a similar case in the same way as marble does. But just as the marble statue refrains from using its eyes and ears, even so a man should avoid every occasion of sin.

You argue that the sight and the company of woman have been found to be inimical to self-restraint and are therefore to be avoided. The argument is fallacious. *Brahmacharya* hardly deserves the name if it can be observed only by avoiding the company of women even when such company is kept with a view to serve. It amounts to physical renunciation unbacked by the essential mental detachment, and lets us down in critical times.

— *The Diary of Mahadev Desai,* Navajivan Publishing House, Ahmedabad, p. 80.

Admittedly, as an objective of humanism, Gandhi considers self-restraint as one of the guiding principles of life. The *brahmachari* endeavouring at *brahmacharya* observes this as a strategy for pure humanism. The dispassionate attitude towards all sensual objects or events of life that a *brahmachari* maintains with strictness of perfection divulges the truth that a man's life should always be directed towards greater values of humanism. Even when sensualism produces an aroma of attachment, the real humanist laughs at easy expositions of life in senile sentimentalism. The real humanist is always an iconoclast.

Perhaps in delineating with the objectives and strategies of humanism, Gandhi comes nearer to Swami Vivekananda who also emphasises on the role of detachment and self-restraint in human endeavour :

Be, therefore, not a beggar; be unattached. This is the most terrible task of life ! You do not calculate the dangers on the path. Even by intellectually recognising the difficulties, we really do not know them until we feel them. From a distance we may get a general view of a part; well, what of that ? We feel and really know it what we are in it. Even if our every attempt is a failure, and we bleed and are torn asunder, yet, through all this, we have to preserve our heart — we must assert our God-head in the midst of all these difficulties. Nature wants us to react, to return blow for blow, cheating for cheating, lie for lie, to hit back with all our might. Then it requires a super divine power not to hit back, to keep control, to be unattached.

I know the difficulties tremendous they are, and ninety per cent of us become discouraged and lose heart, and in our turn, often become pessimists and cease to believe in sincerity, love and all that is grand and noble. So, we find men who in the freshness of their lives have been forgiving, kind, simple, and guileless, become, in old age lying masks of man. Their minds are a mass of intricacy. There may be a good deal of external policy, possibly. They are not hot-heads, they do not speak. They do not curse, nor become angry; but it would be better for them to be able to be angry, a thousand times better, to be able to curse. They cannot. There is death in the heart, for cold hands have seized upon it, and it can no more act, even to utter a curse, even to use a harsh word.

> All this we have to avoid; therefore, I say, we require super-divine power.
>
> — Swami Vivekananda : *The Complete Works of Swami Vivekananda,* Mayavati Memorial Edition, Advaita Ashrama. Vol. II, pp. 89.

The yearning for a super-divine power to combat against evil forces of mankind as set forth in the words of Swami Vivekananda is also the outcome of the objectives and strategies of Gandhian humanism. He also emphasises on a sound character for a sound man to be worthy of mankind. In fact, purity of character through self-restraint leads man to the avenue of all round perfection for which he cannot but endlessly strive.

Gandhi makes the objectives of humanism practical and simple in approach. Therefore, the strategic ways and means of these objectives have a far reaching effect upon human personality. While making an indepth approach to the true spirit of *Swadeshi,* he analyses the humanistic role from the standpoint of one's reaction to immediate neighbours as a taskmaster :

> *Q*. Can a man serve his immediate neighbours and yet serve the whole of humanity ? What is the true meaning of 'Swadeshi' ?
>
> *A*. Gandhiji said that the question had been answered by him on the previous evening. He believed in the truth implicitly

> that man could serve his neighbours and humanity at the same time, the condition being that the service of the neighbours was in no way selfish or exclusive, i.e. did not in any way involve the exploitation of any other human being. The neighbours would then understand the spirit on which such service was given. They would also know that they would be expected to give their service to their neighbours. Thus considered, it would spread like the proverbial snowball gathering strength in geometrical progression encircling the whole earth.
>
> It followed that *Swadeshi* was that spirit which dictated man to serve his next-door neighbours to the exclusion of any other. The condition that he had already mentioned was that the neighbour thus served had in his turn to serve his own neighbours. In this sense *Swadeshi* was never exclusive. It recognised the scientific limitation in human capacity for service.
>
> — Nirmal Kumar Bose : *Selections From Gandhi*, Navajivan Publishing House, Ahmedabad, 1968, pp. 120-121.

The strategic principle of humanism by observing the true spirit of *Swadeshi* by means of good service to neighbours as pointed out by Gandhi also ensures the fact that the ideal of humanism must be soaked in the stream of love and sympathy. As an ideal objective of humanism, love acts as an inherent force of affection and sympathy. The instinctive urge for endearing others as one's very own is the greatest virtue of man as man. Gandhi's own feeling of humanism is noteworthy :

> If I were a perfect man, I own, I should not feel the miseries of neighbours as I do. As a perfect man I should take note of them, prescribe a remedy, and compel adoption by the force of unchallengeable Truth in me. But as yet I only see as through a glass darkly and therefore have to carry conviction by slow and laborious processes, and, then, too, not always with success. . . . I would be less human if, with all my knowledge of the avoidable misery pervading the land. . . . I

did not feel with and for all the suffering of the dumb millions of India.

— Pyarelal : *Mahatma Gandhi : The Last Phase,* Navajivan Publishing House Vol. II, p. 324 .

The inherent spirit of humanism as Gandhi believes, lies in endearing one and all — *Vasudhaiva kutumbakam* — irrespective of caste, creed, community, colour, race, religion etc. The inconsistencies and absence of harmony born of hatred and ill-feeling towards humanity destroy the very essence of humanism. The ideal humanist, as Gandhi himself proves, upholds the spirit of love and truth under any circumstances. As he boldly asserts:

> There can be no room for untruth in my writings, because it is my unshakable belief that there is no religion other than truth and because I am capable of rejecting aught obtained at the cost of truth. My writings cannot but be free from hatred towards any individual because it is my firm belief that it is love that sustains the earth. There only is life where there is love, life without love is death. Love is the reverse of the coin of which the obverse is truth. It is my firm faith . . . that we can conquer the whole world by truth and love.

— R.K. Prabhu & U.R. Rao (compiled) : *The Mind of Mahatma Gandhi,* Oxford University Press, London 1945, p. 21.

As a strategic principle of humanism, love takes a vital role in bringing about goodness in humanity. It is, if purely and sincerely dealt with, turned into religion — the religion that forms the inner essence of humanity. Gandhi calls this religion as the religion of love and truth.

While explaining the inherent characteristics of our desires and motives, Gandhi upholds 'the good of mankind' as the foundation of our morality and religion. As he remarks,

> Our desires and motives may be divided into two classes — selfish and unselfish. All selfish desires are immoral, while the desire to improve ourselves for the sake of doing good to others is truly moral. The highest moral law is that we should

unremittingly work for the good of mankind.

> — M.K. Gandhi : *Ethical Religion*, S. Ganesan, Triplicane, Madras 1930, p. 36.

The efflorescence of humanism becomes possible when there is, as Gandhi points out above, 'the desire to improve ourselves for the sake of doing good to others'. How to be worthy of this spirit of humanism that ultimately serves as a focus of religion ? According to Gandhi, it is nearness to man — a certain sense of deep kinship with mankind — that glorifies humanism, and for that end in view, religion. In his words,

> I could not be leading a religious life unless I identified myself with the whole of mankind, and that I could not to unless I took part in politics. The whole gamut of man's activities today constitutes an indivisible whole. You cannot divide social, economic, political and purely religious work into watertight compartments. I do not know any religion apart from human activity. It provides a moral basis to all other activities which they would otherwise lack, reducing life to a maze of 'sound and fury signifying nothing'.
>
> — R. K. Prabhu & U.R. Rao : *The Mind of Mahatma Gandhi*, (compiled), Oxford University Press, London, 1945, p. 71.

The spirit of humanism should have its exposure everywhere; even politics necessitates an embrace of humanistic endeavour. As a strategic avenue of the exposure of humanism, Gandhi himself makes harmonious blend of politics and religion that makes room for manifestation of the humanistic traits of personality :

> For me, politics bereft of religion are absolute dirt, ever to be shunned. Politics concern nations and that which concerns the welfare of the nations must be one of the concerns of a man who is religiously inclined, in other words, a seeker after God and Truth. For me God and Truth are convertible terms, and if anyone told me that God was a God of untruth or a God of torture, I would decline to worship Him. Therefore, in politics

> also we have to establish the kingdom of Heaven.
>
> —*Ibid.* p. 70.

To be a true humanist, the role of an individual should, as Gandhi thinks, be that of an ardent follower of Truth. Any activity must be assessed in terms of Truth, for Truth alone triumphs over all odds and evils in this world. The Truth that yields no constructive power in mankind fails to impress upon the nobler visions of an individual.

As a strategic policy of humanism, Gandhi gives priority to Truth from another very important aspect. It is to safeguard one's morality which acts and reacts upon experiences encountered. Normally every act of mankind is pre-supposed with the doctrines of constraints and mysteries. The humanistic approach to every item of experience admits the fact that nothing comes to a blob if worthily directed towards the all-round goodness of mankind. The real humanist views every experience an added endeavour for betterment of excellence.

Gandhi goes a step ahead in his strategic viewpoints of humanism. Prior to launching every action related to the welfare of humanity, he categorically denies any distinction between caste and religion and nationality and so on. The World Family of Mankind is the keynote of his objective and essence of humanism.

Explaining the role of his humanistic endeavour to liberate India from the British yoke, Gandhi ventilates his world-view of humanism very explicitly in the A.I.C.C. Resolution adopted at Bombay, September 15, 1940 :

> I do not want England to be defeated or humiliated. It hurts me to find the St. Paul's Cathedral damaged. It hurts me as much as I would be hurt if I heard that the Kashi Visvanath Temple or the Jumma Masjid was damaged. I would like to defend both the Kashi Visvanath Temple and the Jumma Masjid and even the St. Paul's cathedral with my life, but would not take a single life for their defence. That is my fundamental difference with the British people. My sympathy is there with them nevertheless. Let there be no mistake on the part of Englishmen. Congressmen or others, whom my voice reaches, as to where my sympathy lies. It is not because I love the British nation and hate the German. I do not think that the

> Germans as a nation are any worse. We are all tarred with the same brush; we are all members of the vast human family. I decline to draw any distinctions. I cannot claim any superiority for the Indians. We have the same virtues and the same vices. Humanity is not divided into watertight compartments, so that we can go from one to another. They may occupy one thousand rooms, but they are all related to one another. I would not say, 'India should be all in all, let the whole world perish ! That is not my message. India should be all in all, consistently with the well-being of other nations of the world. I can keep India intact, and its freedom also intact only if I have the goodwill towards the whole of the human family which inhabits this little spot of the earth called India.
>
> — D.G. Tendulkar : *Mahatma*, Publications Division, Ministry of Information and Broadcasting, Government of India, Vol. V, p. 322.

Unison of universalism and humanism as Gandhi hints at in his strategy for humanistic endeavour and in identifying and explaining the role of India as the harbinger of humanism is a fundamental objective of humanism. True humanism never allows narrowness in ideal or outlook. It never concentrates strategy for national development for bare utilitarian ends in view. As a matter of fact, when Gandhi speaks of non-violence, it basically ventilates the genuine endeavour of goodwill for one and all. Moreover, the humanism as set forth in the pattern of work-ethics by him also ensures soundness of character based on the invaluable sense of detachment and dispossession. The fountain of joy that runs in the heart out of the sense of detachment and dispossession brings forth a sense of fulfilment that humanism presents mankind. Gandhi's own exposition to this fact substantiates this view :

> When I found myself drawn into the political coil, I asked myself what was necessary for me, in order to remain untouched by immortality, by untruth, by what is known as political gain. I came definitely to the conclusion that, if I had to serve the people in whose midst my life was cast and of whose difficulties I was a witness from day-to-day, I must discard all wealth, all possession.

> I cannot tell you with truth that when the belief come to me, I discarded everything immediately. I must confess to you that progress at first was slow. And now, as I recall those days of struggle, I remember that it was also painful in the beginning. But as days went by I saw that I had to throw overboard many other things which I used to consider as mine, and a time came when it became a matter of positive joy to give up these things. One after another then, by almost geometric progression, things slipped away from me. And, as I am describing my experiences, I can say a great burden fell off my shoulders, and I felt that I could now walk with ease and do my work also in the service of my fellow-men with great comfort and still greater joy. The possession of anything then became a troublesome thing and a burden.
>
> —*Ibid.*, Vol. III, pp. 155.

The quality of detachment as one of the strategies of humanism amply contributes to enrichment of character. It paves avenues for attainment of joy pure, simple and serene. Gandhi emphasises on dispossession and detachment to be equipped with the force of endless endeavour for the good of mankind however insignificant and meagre it might appear.

One of the fundamental objectives of humanism, as Gandhi proves in practice, is, therefore, a search within to be of maximum use to mankind. To do good to others presupposes the fact that one must be as much pure and perfect in mind and heart as possible. Gandhi makes the strategy clear when he remarks,

> It is not for us to find fault with anyone else and sit in judgement over him. We should not be exhausted judging ourselves only, and so long as we notice a single fault in ourselves and wish our relations and friends not to forsake us in spite of such fault, we have no right to poke our nose into other people's conduct. If in spite of ourselves we notice another's fault, we should ask him himself if we have the power and think it proper to do so, but we have no right to ask anybody else.
>
> — Mahadev Desai : *The Diary of Mahadev Desai*, Navajivan Publishing House, Ahmedabad, 1953, p. 98.

To ask and reask oneself before taking others to task, to renew one's conduct with the self-disciplined dynamic force inherent in oneself and to be always in the desire for doing good to others are, according to Gandhi, some of the essential strategies of exercise of humanism. How to adopt these strategies successfully ? What are the easiest but most effective means for translating the objectives of humanism ? The answer, as Gandhi experiments, is to steadfastly follow truth and non-violence. Then the desirable fruit of humanism will automatically be achieved in course of a dynamic and vibrant spirit of human endeavour. As he explicitly observes:

> All universal rules of conduct known as God's commandments are simple and easy to understand and to carry out, if the will is there. They only appear to be difficult because of the inertia which governs mankind. There is nothing at a standstill in nature. Only God is motionless for He was, is and will be the same yesterday, today and tomorrow, and yet is ever moving. . . . Hence I hold that if mankind is to live, it has to come increasingly under sway of truth and non-violence.
>
> — Pyarelal : *Mahatma Gandhi : The Last Phase,* Navajivan Publishing House, Ahmedabad Vol. II, p. 442.

The loving sacrifice of one's little interests and the sense of constructive goodness for mankind are the telling strategies of humanism. Gandhi boldly asserts that one equipped with such type of humanism would freely negotiate with untoward forces anywhere and everywhere. The strategies of non-violence for bringing about a change in human conduct as set forth by him work exceedingly well because the aggression of any offence gets a severe jolt by being bereft of any possibility for retaliation. Gandhi's easy and practical exposition is as follows :

> . . . . let us consider for a moment the inanimate objects. He will surely break his head, who strikes it against a stone. But supposing a stone comes against us through space, we can escape it by stepping aside, or if there is nowhere to step aside, we can bravely stay where we are and receive the stone. That will mean minimum injury and, in case it proves fatal,

> the death will not be as painful as it would be, if we made an effort to ward it off.
>
> Extend the thought a little further, and it is easy to see that, if a senseless man is left alone and no one tries to resist him, he is sure to exhaust himself. Indeed, it is not quite inconceivable that loving sacrifice of many may bring an insane man to senses. Instances are not wanting of absolutely insane people having come back to their senses.
>
> — D. G. Tendulkar : *Mahatma*, Publications Division, Ministry of Information and Broadcasting, Government of India, Vol. V, p. 307.

To be controlled in one's own temperaments and attitudes and to be a real sympathiser to the woes and sufferings of mankind necessitate a continual striving for the qualities of harmony and self-restraint that Gandhi sincerely advocates as working strategies for efflorescence of humanism.

As one of the components of self-restraint and self-denial, Gandhi introduced fasting in the Tolstoy Farm. The inherent purpose is to awaken the sense of sympathy and purity of humanism in mankind by control of passion and selfish attitudes. He prescribes this exercise of fasting for self-control as one of the strategies for manifestation of humanism and defends it with the armour of one of the great sayings from the *Bhagavadgita*. In his own words,

> Fasting can help to curb animal passion, only if it is undertaken with a view to self-restraint. Some of my friends have actually found their animal passion and palate stimulated as an after-effect of fasts. That is to say, fasting is futile unless it is accompanied by an incessant longing for self-restraint. The famous verse from the second chapter of *Bhagavadgita* is worth noting in this connection :
>
> > 'For a man who is fasting his senses outwardly, the sense-objects disappear. Leaving the yearning behind; but when He has seen the Highest, Even the yearning disappears'.
>
> — M. K. Gandhi : *An Autobiography*, Navajivan Publishing House, Ahmedabad, p. 245.

Gandhi also warns that mere physical fasting would contribute very little to awaken the inherent spirit of humanism. He, therefore, emphasises on mental fasting as a supplementary strategy for self-restraint to avert untoward disaster of humanism:

> Fasting and similar discipline is, therefore, one of the means to the end of self-restraint, but it is not all, and if physical fasting is accompanied by mental fasting, it is bound to end in hypocrisy and disaster.
>
> —*Ibid.* p. 245.

What is the inherent force that strengthens the components of humanism already in mankind ? According to Gandhi, it is service towards humanity by means of elimination of the fruit of service one normally hankers after. That any service to humanity is, in fact, service to oneself is the implicit strategy that man actually undertakes as a part of renunciation. As Gandhi poignantly observes,

> To serve without desire is to favour not others, but ourselves, even as in discharging a debt we serve only ourselves, lighten our burden and fulfil our duty. Again, not only the good, but all of us are bound to place our resources at the disposal of humanity. The duty of renunciation differentiates mankind from the beast,
>
> — M. K. Gandhi : *From Yeravda Mandir,* Navajivan Publishing House, Ahmedabad, p. 81.

Taking all practicalities into consideration, Gandhi also hints at the fact that to be self-restraint, one cannot but embrace violence and hatred which are unavoidable consequences of day-to-day life. To deny this fact is to deny the progress of humanism. It is, therefore, necessary to continually strive for elimination of the self for the well-being of humanity. In the words of Gandhi,

> *Ahimsa* is a comprehensive principle. We are helpless mortals caught in the conflagration of *himsa.* The saying that life lives on life has a deep meaning in it. Man cannot for a moment live without consciously for unconsciously committing

> outward *himsa*. The very fact of his living — eating, drinking and moving about — necessarily involves some *himsa*, destruction of life, be it ever so minute. A votary of *ahimsa* therefore remains true to his faith if the spring of all his actions is compassion, if he shuns to the best of his ability the destruction of the tiniest creature, tries to save it, and thus incessantly strives to be free from the deadly coil of *himsa*. He will be constantly growing in self-restraint and compassion, but he can never become entirely free from outward *himsa*.
>
> Then again, because underlying *ahimsa* is the unity of all life, the error of one cannot but affect all, and hence man cannot be wholly free from *himsa*, so long as he continues to be a social being, he cannot but participate in the *himsa* that the very existence of society involves. When two nations are fighting, the duty of votary of *ahimsa* is to stop the war. He who is not equal to that duty, he who has no power of resisting war, he who is not qualified to resist war, may take part in war, and yet whole-heartedly try to free himself, his nation and the world from war.
>
> — M. K. Gandhi : *An Autobiography*, Navajivan Publishing House, Ahmedabad, pp. 257-58.

Does this mean that as a strategy for nursling the seeds of humanism within ourselves none of us can tread on the path of pure *ahimsa* or non-violence ? If not, what should be our approach to humanism from the standpoint of *ahimsa* ? Gandhi's reply is :

> . . . If we have a clear conception of it (pure *ahimsa*) and have a living faith in its matchless efficacy, it will not be found to be so hard to practise as it is sometimes supposed to be. It will be well to remember the immortal Mahabharata verse in this connection. The seer poet therein proclaims loudly to the whole world that *dharma* includes within itself both legitimate *artha* and *kama*, and asks why men do not follow the royal road of *dharma* that leads to both earthly and spiritual bliss. *Dharma* here does not signify the mere observance of externals. It signifies the way of truth and non-violence. The scriptures have given us two immortal

maxims. One of the maxims is this : '*Ahimsa* is the supreme law of *dharma*'. And the other is : 'There is no other law or *dharma* than truth'. These two maxims provide us the key to all lawful *artha* and *karma*. Why should we then hesitate to act up to them ? Strange as it may appear, the fact remains that people find the easiest of things oftentimes to be the most difficult to follow. The reason, to borrow a term from the science of physics lies in inertia. The physicists tell us that inertia is an essentially, and in its own place, a most useful quality of matter. It is that alone which steadies the universe and prevents it from flying off at a tangent. But for it, the latter would be a chaos of motion. Inertia becomes an incubus and a vice, when it ties the mind down to old ruts. It is this kind of inertia, which is responsible for our rooted prejudice that to practise pure *ahimsa* is difficult. It is up to us to get rid of this incubus. The first step in this direction is firmly to resolve that all untruth and *himsa* shall hereafter be taboo to us, whatever sacrifice it might seem to involve. For, the good these may seem to achieve is in appearance only, but in reality it is deadly poison. If our resolve is firm and our conviction is clear, it would mean half the battle is won, and the practice of these two qualities would come comparatively easy to us.

— M. K. Gandhi : *Harijan*, July 13, 1940, Quoted in D. G. Tendulkar : *Mahatma*, Publications Division, Ministry of Information and Broadcasting, Government of India, Vol. V, pp. 305-306.

Admittedly, the overcome the shortcomings within each one of us is to follow pure *ahimsa* gradually but effectively, and, in consistently doing so, we can heighten the spirit of humanism within ourselves. The point crucial and delicate, of course, is how to identify the marks of improvement or betterment of strategies to be chalked out and applied? Mere self-evaluation might be an easy pray to excessive subjectivity. Again, too much of objectivity might eight shy of appropriate appreciation to humanistic endeavour since all qualities of head and heart more often than not shake hands with subjective interpretation.

Moreover, as Gandhi lays more stress on individual endeavour that ultimately leads to group endeavour, to the welfare of one and all, the desirable strategies of humanism must primarily encompass ensured proficiencies in every individual. Since the goal of humanism is to enable every individual to be conscious of his qualities and limitations, Gandhian humanism looks upon the gradual upbringing of an individual the keypoint of a global humanistic environment. A sense of moral awakening ably supported by aesthetic sensibilities goes a long way in the fulfilment of any strategy undertaken for emergence of humanism. The qualities that contribute to aesthetic sensibilities truly denoting or representing humanism are also ones promoting excellence of mankind. Modesty, sincerity and other allied qualities contributing to humanism are greatly highlighted in Gandhian humanism. They act as resourceful strategies for exposure of humanism. They act and react against undesirable behavioural designs of mankind and serve as effective antidotes to selfishness, hatred etc. Explaining the role of humility as an effective strategy inherent in non-co-operation, Gandhi observes :

> A non-co-operator is nothing if he is not humble. When self-satisfaction creeps over a man, he has ceased to grow and therefore has become unfit for freedom. He who offers a little sacrifice from a lowly and religious spirit quickly realises the littleness of it. Once on the path of sacrifice, we find out the measure of our selfishness and must continually wish to give more and not be satisfied till there is a complete self-surrender.
>
> — M. K. Gandhi : *Young India*, September 29, 1921, p. 306.

Gandhian humanism demands for its objective such type of humility born out of self-surrender by means of persuing simplicity and sacrifice in every affair of life. It might, for the time being, bring forth defeat but ultimately it will direct towards eternal victory of mankind.

The intrinsic value of the objectives and strategies of Gandhian humanism is undeniably endless. The philosophy that works as a strategic force of humanism is to continually purify oneself in course of one's duty towards oneself and to others around. Moreover, with devotion to such type of responsibility to become truly humanistic, erosion of limitations and weaknesses within oneself becomes a thrilling and pulsating challenge. It is a march ever onward for advancement of humanism. It is, again, a march to see God face-to-face and to see within oneself.

Admitting his own limitations, Gandhi explains the above concept of humanism as follows :

> All I claim for myself is, that I am incessantly trying to overcome every one of my weaknesses. I have attained great capacity, I believe, for suppressing and curbing my senses, but I have not become incapable of sin, i.e., of being acted upon by my senses. I believe it to be possible for every human being to attain that blessed and indescribable sinless state in which he feels within himself the presence of God to the exclusion of everything else. It is, I must confess, as yet a distant scene. And therefore, it is not possible for me to show the nation a present way to complete non-violence, in practice.
>
> —*Ibid.*, November 17, 1921, p. 367.

Perhaps the above frank confession gives birth to sincerity of purpose that contributes a great deal towards dissemination of humanism. Every bit of earnest endeavour to accomplish any activity, however apparently insignificant, serves as a stepping stone to exposure of humanism in steadfastness to truth and purity. In this connection, one might recall the invaluable words of advice voiced forth by Gandhi in order to be genuinely humanistic in discharging one's duties :

> No matter how insignificant the thing you have to do, do it as well as you can, give it as much of your care and attention as you would give to the thing your regard as most important. For it will be by those small things that you shall be judged.
>
> — M. K. Gandhi : *Harijan*, July 27, 1935, p. 191.

An apostle of eternal humanism, Gandhi upholds the worth of humanity in terms of little acts of immense importance.

When will global humanism be immuned with the Gandhian strategies of humanistic endeavour ?

3

RELIGION AND HUMANISM : Gandhian Guidelines

THE INNER world of man is unfathomable. It is an incomparable wonderland of wills and aspirations, askance and curiosity, agonies and ecstasies. The man who controls his passions and wills, receives within himself the reward of the creation of a poem — a poem of fulfilment towards the greater worth of perfection. He ceases to think about himself and beings to think more about others living or non-being, little or great. To him everything appears as a challenge to re-discover himself by means of benevolence and magnanimity. Everything turns into a test for poignance and perfection.

The core of humanism in a man is thus born. The function of humanism in him starts as soon as he is born in this world, looks around with wonderful eyes and kicks in the air to indicate his restlessness for his debt to the Mother Earth with all her inhabitants.

With this sense of indebtedness, man seeks salvation (*Moksha*) from the limitations of service towards himself and others for the service of God. In fact, his inward search, endless and profound, determines how far he is faithful to himself, to religion, to God and to morality. Gandhi explains this role of an individual as self-realisation which is religion in terms of morality which ultimately turns out to be the mouthpiece of humanism. Explaining this objective of life in course of his introduction to autobiography, he categorically observes :

> What I want to achieve, — What I have been striving and pining to achieve these thirty years, — is self-realisation, to see God face to face, to attain *Moksha*. I live and move and have my being in pursuit of this goal. All that I do by way of speaking and writing, and all my venture in the political field, are directed to this same end. But as I have all along believed that what is possible for one is possible for all, my

> experiments have not been conducted in the closet, but in the open; and I do not think that this fact detracts from their spiritual value. There are some things which are known only to oneself and one's Maker. These are clearly incommunicable. The experiments I am about to relate are not such. But they are spiritual, or rather moral; for the essence of religion is morality.
>
> — M. K. Gandhi : *An Autobiography*, Navajivan Publishing House, Ahmedabad, p. XIV.

Bearing in mind all the time the truth that the aim of life is to ceaselessly try to find out goodness and nurture it against all odds, Gandhi banks heavily upon morality that serves as a guideline to his concept of religion. Self-purification in the essence of goodness thus takes a major role in being truly religious and humane in spirit and temperament. As he frankly observes,

> I know, too, that I shall never know God if I do not wrestle with and against evil even at the cost of life itself. I am fortified in the belief of my own humble and limited experience. The purer I try to become the nearer to God I feel myself to be. How much more should I be near to Him when my faith is not a mere apology, as it is today, but has become as immovable as the Himalayas and as white and bright as the snows on their peaks?
>
> — R. K. Prabhu & U. R. Rao (compiled) : *The Mind of Mahatma Gandhi*, Oxford University Press, London, 1945, p. 22.

The guiding principle of every religious thought as Gandhi poignantly feels and practises in action, is transcendence. That it is always applicable for purification of mankind in all his thoughts and activities, makes it worthy of its connotation. The moral instincts of mankind are, therefore, surcharged best by the religious sensibilities that empower every human being to transcend. In this connection, Gandhi's own explanation of religion might be recalled :

> Let me explain what I mean by religion. It is not the Hindu

> religion which I certainly prize above all other religions, but the *religion* which transcends Hinduism, which changes one's very nature, which binds one indissolubly to the truth within and which ever purifies. It is the permanent element in human nature which counts no cost too great in order to find full expression and which leaves the soul utterly restless until it has found itself, known its Maker and appreciated the true correspondence between the Maker and itself.
>
> — M. K. Gandhi : *Young India*, May 12, 1920.

The religion as explained above by Gandhi makes a marriage of religion and humanism. It also ensures the fact that a living faith in self-realisation ultimately brushes aside all incoherences of humanity and leads one towards grater spiritual height. The limitations of humanity are those erroneously termed as religious sacrifices through immoral sanctions of mankind. Gandhi wants to shatter all disillusions and misconceptions of religion by means of ardent endeavour to withdraw ourselves from our innumerable limitations in order to be able to hear 'the divine music' continually going on amidst and within ourselves :

> Indeed, even the so-called realisation has at bottom an element of faith without which it cannot be sustained. In the very nature of things if must be so. Who can transgress the limitations of his being ? I hold that complete realisation is impossible in this embodied life. Nor it is necessary. A living immovable faith is all that is required for catching the full spiritual height attainable by human beings. God is not outside this earthly case of ours. Therefore, exterior proof is not of much avail, if any at all. We must ever fail to perceive him through the senses, because He is beyond them. We can feel Him, if we will but withdraw ourselves from the senses. The divine music is incessantly going on within ourselves, but the loud senses drown the delicate music, which is unlike and infinitely superior to anything we can perceive or bear with our senses.
>
> — R. K. Prabhu & U. R. Rao (compiled) : *The Mind of Mahatma Gandhi*, O.U.P., London, 1945, pp. 22-23.

True religion and, for that end in view, true, resourceful, living humanism is always indicative of 'the divine music' or the delicate music going on ceaselessly within ourselves. Gandhi advocates for a beyonding of our senses primarily because purity of the self is the most desirable and necessary factor for beyonding of the senses and nearness to God , Moreover, with the inherent urge for the beyonding of the senses, we are what we should be as the true followers of religion. Our earnest commitments and endeavours for self-purification is nothing but our sincere strivings for self-realisation which means that we are on the right track of humanism. The ills of mankind are, in fact, the ones of self-being continually neglected or ignored. Sometimes the self is belittled, too. The errors of humanity are the offshoots of this belittled self. 'The divine music' taught or preached by every religion terribly suffers from such type of belittled attitude. The agonies of the lost soul and the self are, indeed, the agonies of humanism and religion.

Gandhi calls for a reorientation of the self through action in purity and perfection and not simply by means of contemplation. His religion is the religion of action aiming at complete realisation of the self. His religion is also the religion of the beyonding of the senses. Then, and then only, the lost music of humanity can be revived and heard again.

Apart from the fact that self-realisation necessitates detachment from ordinary and commonplace source of enjoyment, Gandhi clarifies his points of view of humanism synchronised in the holy thoughts of religion. One of the fundamental avenues of this synchronisation as Gandhi shows in action is the religion of love, the most desirable aspect of humanism. The strategies of *ahimsa* or non-violence as he follows and advises everyone to follow, are nothing but identification with every living force responding and representing God. This concept of religion is undoubtedly a significant point of departure from the stereotyped concept of God, which comes closest to that of Sri Ramakrishna or Swami Vivekananda. It is also the inherent call of every religion to love every living being anywhere and everywhere. Love as the essence of self-purification as Gandhi believes, heightens humanism. This is not all. Love, as a powerful component of religion and humanism, spreads like the sweet fragrance of flowers all throughout. In the words of Gandhi,

> To see the universal and all-pervading Spirit of Truth face to fact one must be able to love the meanest of creation as

> oneself. And a man who aspires after that cannot afford to keep out of any field of life. That is why my devotion to truth has drawn me into the field of politics; and I can say without the slightest hesitation, and yet in all humility, that those who say that religion has nothing to do with politics do not know what religion means.
>
> — M. K. Gandhi : *An Autobiography*, Navajivan Publishing House, Ahmedabad, 14, p. 615.

How can one identify oneself with every living being ? Gandhi has a very categorical answer :

> Identification with everything that lives is impossible without self-purification; without self-purification the observance of the law of *ahimsa* must remain an empty dream; God can never be realised by one who is not pure of heart. Self-purification therefore must mean purification in all walks of life. And purification of oneself necessarily leads to the purification of one's surroundings.
>
> —*Ibid.* pp. 615-616.

For purity of heart achieved through self-realisation, Gandhi considers humanism a matter of belonging to oneself to be true to others. This is the only religion that serves mankind best. Since religion is to equip one to be of utmost service towards the good of mankind, it is necessary that one gradually prepares oneself for the best service to be rendered towards mankind. The moral force that acts as Gandhi ardently feels, is the great Upanishadic saying : *Aa noh bhadra kratava yantu visvatah* — let noble-thoughts come to us from every direction. The source of eternal strength lies in learning, identifying and actualising the noble thoughts that would serve best for the all-round development and welfare of mankind.

When Gandhi emphasises on prayer, he practically lays stress on peace and orderliness of mind for the welfare of the entire humanity. He also looks upon prayer to bring together all the evils of humanity to be recast in the power of man's inherent force to turn all evil into goodness. This sense of humanism becomes alive and all powerful when one wholeheartedly associates oneself for the service towards fellowmen. As Gandhi characteristically highlights,

> We are born to serve our fellowmen, and we cannot properly do so unless we are wide awake. There is an eternal struggle raging in Man's breast between the powers of darkness and of light, and he who has not the sheet-anchor of prayer to rely upon will be a victim to the powers of darkness. The man of prayer will be at peace with himself and with the whole world, the man who goes about the affairs of the world without a prayerful heart will be miserable and will make the world also miserable. Apart therefore from its bearing on man's condition after death, prayer has incalculable value for man in this world of the living. Prayer is the only means of bringing about orderliness and peace and repose in our daily acts.
>
> — M K. Gandhi : *Young India*, January 23, 1930, p. 26.

The religion that should sincerely play its role in the life of mankind is the religion of all-round human welfare. This religion, as Gandhi firmly believes knows no defeat and does not, under any circumstances, compromise with evil forces. This religion is above fear and vicissitudes and it boldly encounters every undesirable force against humanism. It only seeks strength in one's faith in the All-Loving who never betrays love to be re-equipped with the power of doing good to mankind.

The failures on the part of an individual to combat against evil forces can easily be surmounted if he believes in the omnipresence of God in every affair of life. An uncompromising faith in God is the great divine assistance that he receives at every time and on every occasion makes the onward journey of man for self-realisation smooth and successful. From his broad religious view of humanism, Gandhi visualises God who is always at one's beck and call :

> God is the hardest taskmaster I have known on earth, and He tries you through and through. And when you find that your faith is failing or your body is failing you, and you are sinking, He comes to your assistance somehow or other and proves to you that you must not lose your faith and that He is always at your beck and call, but on His terms, and not on

your terms.

— M. K. Gandhi : *Speeches and Writings of Mahatma Gandhi*, G. A. Natesan & Co. Madras, p. 1069.

Aiming at religion for understanding and efflorescence of humanism is an eternal dimension of Indian philosophy. The sense of self-purification as nursled and caressed through the religion of love — the surest way of nearness to mankind — grows in spontaneity with the awareness of global goodness: *Vasudhaiva Kutumbakam*. Keeping in view that everyone is our near and dear one, and everyone has a natural kinship with us, religion makes wide room for efflorescence of humanism. In that case truth and religion become one and the same. Gandhi's own experience reveals this aspect of unison of truth and religion in the form of purity of action and contemplation :

> To see the universal and all-pervading spirit of Truth face to face one must be able to love the meanest of creation as oneself. Identification with everything that lives is impossible without self-purification and God can never be realised by one who is not pure in heart.
>
> — M. K. Gandhi : *An Autobiography*, Navajivan Publishing House, Ahmedabad, 1940, p. 615.

For identification with all living beings, whatever guidance an individual receives out of his self-conscience and self-purification paves avenues of true religion and true humanism. The task for self-preparation is the task that Gandhi in his own religious concept terms as *tapasya*. It is the task of self-conditioning by means of self-suffering for the good of humanity. Let Truth emerge from the darkness of ignorance and impurity. Let the light of wisdom based on or rather enkindled with love enlighten the world of littleness. Truth alone stands out as the supreme criterion of religion and humanism. It sets all things in the right direction and to set all things in the right direction by means of Truth is the great lesson or religion yet to be learnt. In fact, Gandhi substitutes God by Truth, and when be does so he makes a broader dimension of religion in the light of humanism :

> . . . Truth is the right designation of God. Hence there is

> nothing wrong in everyone following Truth according to his lights. Indeed it is his duty to do so. Then if there is a mistake on the part of anyone so fellowing Truth, it will be automatically set right. For the quest of Truth involves *tapas* — self-suffering sometimes even unto death. There can be no place in it for even a trace of self-interest. In such selfless search for Truth nobody can lose his bearings for long. Directly he takes to the wrong path he stumbles, and is thus re-directed to the right path.
>
> — M. K. Gandhi : *From Yeravda Mandir*, Navajivan Press, Ahmedabad, 1935, p.4.

The pursuit of Truth on the part of an individual is to redirect oneself, as Gandhi rightly believes, to the path of humanism. The inner conscience that alerts him to be true to himself in order to be true to others is the source-point of humanism. For this, he needs a preparation, a sacrifice, a *tapasya*, a meditation within. This preparation or sacrifice, *tapasya* or meditation within eliminates all narrowness of vision and heralds the glory of altruism which is the essence of humanism. Gandhi himself wavers from the charge of autocracy often unfortunately labelled against him by sharing his spirit of conscience and freedom and by holding himself beyond petty religious sensibilities for the noble cause of goodness of mankind by means of the pursuit of Truth or non-violence. As he defends,

> I have never been able to subscribe to the charge of obstinacy or autocracy. On the contrary, I pride myself on my yielding nature in non-vital matters. I detest autocracy. Valuing my freedom and independence I equally cherish them for others. I have no desire to carry a single soul with me if I cannot appeal to his or her reason. My unconventionality I carry to the point of rejecting the divinity of the oldest Shastras if they cannot convince my reason. But I have found by experience that, if I wish to live in society and still retain my independence, I must limit the points of utter independence to matters of first rate importance. In all others which do not involve a departure from one's personal religion or moral code, one must yield to the majority.
>
> — M. K. Gandhi : *Young India*, July 14, 1920.

Like an ideal humanist, Gandhi believes in the rational approach to Truth from the standpoint of altruism. The inherent strength of Truth to hold the spirit of humanism above all untoward circumstances consolidates personality and character. Truth as an internal force of every action sublimates the evil and boosts whatever is good for mankind. Therein lies the point of unison between humanism and religion, and true religion always appeals and appreciates the great Upanishadic doctrine : *Sarve Sukhino bhavantu* (let everyone of us be happy). Religion, then, merges in the invaluable spirit of human welfare. Gandhi extends his viewpoints on religion to politics also, for he thinks that true politics is always an introspective endeavour to the cause of humanism and, therefore, it must have its basis on Truth and religion. As he remarks,

> I could not live for a single second without religion. Many of my political friends despair of me because they say that even my politics is derived from religion. And they are right. My politics and all other activities of mine are derived from my religion. I go further and say that every activity of a man of religion must be derived from his religion, because religion means being bound to God, that is to say God rules your every breath.
>
> — R. K. Prabhu & U. R. Rao (compiled) : *The Mind of Mahatma Gandhi,* Oxford University Press, London, 1945, p. 70.

For an ideal setting of 'the kingdom of Heaven' in politics, Gandhi makes an ideal and unified platform of cohesion among politics, religion and Truth. As he categorically observes,

> For me, politics bereft of religion are absolute dirt, ever to be shunned. Politics concern nations and that which concerns the welfare of nations must be one of the concerns of a man who is religiously inclined, in other words, a seeker after God and Truth. For me, God and Truth are convertible terms, and if anyone told me that God was a God of untruth or a God of torture, I would decline to worship Him. Therefore, in politics also we have to establish the Kingdom of Heaven.
>
> — *Ibid.*

A living faith in God rather than in sole abstractions comprises the essence of religion and humanism. This activates humanity and everyone becomes rational and dynamic in quest of the All Generous. The belief in the co-existence of God and man as highlighted by Gandhi broadens the vision of unison between religion and humanism. It is this broadening of vision that marks the essence of human civilisation. Gandhi takes recourse to Truth primarily because it is an all-embracing factor of humanism and is never denied even by the atheists. For the role of Truth as a dominant factor of religion and humanism, his own elucidation deserves a reference :

> No search is possible without some workable assumptions. If we grant nothing, we find nothing. Ever since its commencement, the world, the wise and the foolish included, has proceeded upon the assumption that if we are, God is, and that, if God is not, we are not. And since belief in God is co-existent with the humankind existence of God is treated as a fact more definite that the fact that the sun is. This living faith has solved a large number of puzzles of life. It has alleviated our misery. It sustains us in life, it is our solace in death. The very search for Truth becomes interesting and worthwhile, because of this belief. But Truth is God. God is, because Truth is. We embark upon the search, because we believe that there is Truth and that it can be found by diligent search and meticulous observance of the well-known and well-tried rules of search. There is no record in history of the failure of such search. Even the atheists who have pretended to disbelieve in God have believed in Truth. The trick they have performed is that of giving God another, not a new, name. His names are legion. Truth is the crown of them all.
>
> — D. G. Tendulkar : *Mahatma*, Vithalbhai K. Jhaveri D. G. Tendulkar, Bombay, Vol III, pp 359-60.

While disseminating the view that God who knows no single name or identity but is identified with many a name in order to be one, Gandhi upholds humanism as a process of harmonisation between Truth and religion. In fact, when he speaks of one Religion, be infuses the spirit of tolerance as one of the fundamental components of humanism and accelerates the role of 'True knowledge of religion' to defuse inconsistencies whatsoever. As he characteristically observes,

> We have not realised religion in its perfection, even as we have not realised God. Religion of our conception, being thus imperfect, is always subject to a process of evolution. And if all faiths outlined by men are imperfect, the question of comparative merit does not arise. All faiths constitute a revelation of Truth, but all are imperfect, and liable to error. Reverence for other faiths need not blind us to their faults. We must be keenly alive to the defects of our own faith also, yet not leave it on that account, but try to overcome those defects. Looking at all religions with an equal eye, we would not only not hesitate, but would think it our duty, to blend into our faith every acceptable feature of other faiths.
>
> — M. K. Gandhi : *From Yeravda Mandir*, Navajivan Press, Ahmedabad, 1935, p. 55.

Furthermore, in explaining the synchronising role of tolerance in religion, Gandhi poignantly remarks :

> The one Religion is beyond all speech. Imperfect men put it into such language as they can command, and their words are interpreted by other men equally imperfect. Whose interpretation is to be held to be the right one ? Everybody is right from his own standpoint, but it is not impossible that everybody is wrong. Hence the necessity of tolerance, which does not mean indifference to one's own faith, but a more intelligent and purer love for it. Tolerance gives us spiritual insight, which is as far from fanaticism as the North Pole from the South—True Knowledge of religion breaks down the barriers between faith and faith.
>
> —*Ibid.*

With the humanistic spirit of tolerance that serves as a bridge between Truth and religion, Gandhi advocates for service to fellowmen, that actually determines the ultimate Truth and realisation of the spirit of humanism based on religion. To bring about a proper and desirable harmony of consciousness in our day-to-day living, prayer holds the key to peace and discipline — the two essential components of religion and humanism. Gandhi's introspective viewpoints of the same clarifies the true role of every person to manifest his humane sensibilities in terms of prayer :

> We are born to serve our fellowmen, and we cannot properly do so unless we are wide awake. There is an eternal struggle raging in man's breast between the powers of darkness and of light, and he who has not the sheet-anchor of prayer to rely upon will be a victim to the powers of darkness. The man of prayer will be at peace with himself and with the whole world, the man who goes about the affairs of the world without a prayerful heart will be miserable and will make the world also miserable. Apart therefore from its bearing on man's condition after death, prayer has incalculable value for man in this world of the living. Prayer is the only means of bringing about orderliness and peace and repose in our daily acts.
>
> — M. K. Gandhi : *Young India*, January 23, 1930.

A 'heart search' as prayer is, so appropriately explained by Gandhi, it acts as a guiding force to all humanistic and religious endeavour. And when one talks of self-purification or inward search, prayer stands out as one's supreme entity. It leads to humanity and simplicity, purity and serenity. It also leads to the great truth of every religion that God is omnipresent. Gandhi elucidates the point as follows :

> He (God) is within everyone. Nothing happens without His permission. Our prayer is a heart-search. It is a reminder to ourselves that we are helpless without His support. No effort is complete without prayer, — without a definite recognition that the best human endeavour is of no effect if it has not God's blessing behind. Prayer is a call to humility. It is a call to self-purification, to inward search.
>
> I ask those who appreciate the necessity of inward purification to join in the prayer that we may read the purpose of God in such visitations, that they may humble us and prepare us to face our Maker whenever the call comes, and that we may be ever ready to share the sufferings of our fellows whoever they may be.
>
> — M. K. Gandhi : *Harijan*, June 8, 1935, p. 132.

For inward purification which is an essential component of true religion, Gandhi adds service — service of humanity, for God as he believes, is in man and man alone. His own mission reflects this view-point :

> I am endeavouring to see God through service of humanity, for I know that God is neither in heaven, nor down below, but in everyone.
>
> — R. K. Prabhu & U. R. Rao (compiled) : *The Mind of Mahatma Gandhi*, Oxford University Press, London, 1945, p. 24.

To heighten religion is to ennoble humanity and *vice versa*. It is, therefore, appropriate to uphold religion as a dynamic factor that leads everyone of us to the point of unison. Different opinions on religion are, indeed, different aspects of human endeavour, that converge on point of cohesion. All religions are the assembly of humanistic endeavour happily merged in one out of many dimensions. Gandhi's simple assessment is noteworthy :

> Religions are different roads converging to the same point. What does it matter that we take different roads, so long as we reach the same goal ? In reality, there are as many religions as there are individuals.
>
> — M. K. Gandhi : *Hind Swaraj or Indian Home Rule*, Navajivan Publishing House, Ahmedabad, 1944, p. 24.

That true religion and true humanism are identical in the sense that there is the common objective of transcendence, never averts Gandhi's attention. He, therefore, believes in the transcendence of all religions that eliminate all barriers in the unison of the Maker and man. His concept of religion is entirely merged in the spirit of transcendence and altruism :

> It is not the Hindu religion which I certainly prize above all other religions, but the *religion* which transcends Hinduism, which changes one's very nature, which binds one indissolubly to the truth within and which ever purifies. It is

> the permanent element in human nature which counts no cost too great in order to find full expression and which leaves the soul utterly restless until it has found itself, known to its Maker and appreciates the true correspondence between the Maker and itself.
>
> — M. K. Gandhi : *Young India*, May 12, 1920.

To unfold 'the permanent element in human nature' as true religion is, necessitates ceaseless endeavour in moulding the finer aspect of humanism. As true religion and true morality are, as Gandhi believes, one and the same aspect of humanism and are inseparable, so the mind of every person should be allowed to enjoy freedom in thought and action in order to reveal the poignance of humanism which by itself manifests religion. All good and evil acts are, indeed, the touchstones of morality and ethics *par excellence* and ultimately of religion and humanism. As Gandhi categorically remarks,

> So long as we act like machines, there can be no question of morality. If we want to call an action moral, it should have been done consciously and as a matter of duty. Any action that is dictated by fear or by coercion of any kind ceases to be moral. It also follows that all good deeds that are prompted by hope of happiness in the next world cease to be moral.
>
> — M. K. Gandhi : *Ethical Religion*, S. Ganesan, Madras. 1930, p. 43.

Elsewhere, Gandhi points out the ills of compulsion and states :

> The mind of a man who remains good under compulsion cannot improve, in fact it worsens. And when compulsion is removed all the defects well up to the surface with even greater force.
>
> — M. K. Gandhi : *Harijan*, September 29, 1946, p. 333.

With freedom exercised in humane sensibilities, a man becomes liberal in approach to religion and God. In fact, the concept of God, divergent and manifold, is widened in the light of humanism. Everyone's belief in God is thus honoured and religion gets its true connotation. Gandhi's practical comment on this point is very poignant and remarkable :

> I do not foresee a time when there would be only one religion on earth in practice. In theory, since there is one God, there can be only one religion. But in practice, no two persons I have known have had the same identical conception of God. Therefore, there will, perhaps, always be different religions answering to different temperaments and climatic conditions.
>
> — R. K. Prabhu & U. R. Rao (compiled) : *The Mind of Mahatma Gandhi,* Oxford University Press, London, 1945, p. 84.

All true religion aims at perfection and all true humanism stands for true religion. The spirit of enquiry and fulfilment for Truth thrusts one to be truly humanistic in order to be truly religious. One cannot, therefore, be rest assured with one religious principle naturally because human hunger for perfection in religion and nearness to God drives one to embrace all religion as complementary to each other. This unique approach never narrows or knowingly dishonours any religion but widens and heightens every religion to be eternal and perfect. In the words of Gandhi,

> I believe that all the great religions of the world are true more of less. I say 'more or less' because.I believe that everything the human mind touches, by reason of the very fact that human beings are imperfect, becomes imperfect. Perfection is the exclusive attribute of God and it is indescribable, untranslatable. I do believe that it is possible in every human being to become perfect even as God is perfect. It is necessary for us all to aspire after perfection, but when that blessed state is attained, it becomes indescribable, indefinable and I, therefore, admit, in all humility, that even the Vedas, the Koran and the Bible are imperfect word of God and, imperfect beings that we are, swayed to and fro by a multitude of passions, it is impossible for us even to understand this word

of God in its fullness.

> — R. K. Prabhu & U. R. Rao (compiled) *The Mind of Mahatma Gandhi,* Oxford University Press, London 1945, p. 82.

For an understanding of the highest truth which is also Truth *par excellence,* God acts as a symbol of humanism. Gandhi, therefore, emphasises on service to humanity as service to God. As he observes,

> The immediate service of all human beings becomes a necessary part of the endeavour, simply because the only way to find God is to see Him in His creation and be one with it. This can only be done by service of all. I am a part and parcel of the whole, and I cannot find Him apart from the rest of humanity.
>
> — M. K. Gandhi : *Harijan*, August 29, 1936, p. 226.

Elsewhere, Gandhi expresses the same view of oneness of humanism and religion :

> I believe in absolute oneness of God and, therefore, also of humanity. What though we have many bodies ? We have but one soul. The rays of the sun ar many through refraction. But they have the same source.
>
> — M. K. GAndhi : *Young India,* September 25, 1924, p. 313.

As a *Karmayogi,* a saint dedicated to the service of humanity, Gandhi widens the concept of religion as human endeavour for continual purification of the soul and the self. The individual self as he believes, merges in the universal self to become a worthy expression and exponent of the divine self. This belief in the divine self heightens humanity to the auspicious sense of mutual love to be in unison with the blessings of the divine self within. Gandhi represents and manifests this divine self within till the last moment of his life. As Dr. R. R. Diwakar observes,

> A human being is a bundle or bunch of energies. The soul or self calling itself 'I' is in command, in theory only. Love is one of powerful energies. If a person purifies this energy by diverting it from all other objects and dedicates it entirely to one's own Deity, he becomes a Bhakta, a devotee and Bhakti Yoga is born because the devotee yokes his power of purified love to the service of his Deity. In the case of Gandhi, he realised that this whole creation was at the command of God. He has gone on record to say 'not a leaf moves except by the Will of God'. He names his God, Rama and the presence of Rama in this total consciousness was so vivid and constant that even at the most critical moment of death, his uppermost thought was 'He Ram'.
>
> — Dr. R. R. Diwakar : "Gandhi As A Yogi", *Gandhi Marg*. Gandhi Peace Foundation, New Delhi, Vol X, No. 5, August 1988, p. 282.

A mystic-humanist, Gandhi enkindles the spirit of humanism in the beyonding of religion. He instils a faith eternal that breaks the barriers of littleness often nursed in ignorance. He craves for the purified atmosphere of all mankind, where man finds the wider avenues of pursuit of inner poignance and excellence. When he prays he humbles himself for the glory of man — the glory that is felt inwardly with ceaseless endeavour and endless toil of the human soul.

Meanwhile, let us ask ourselves: Are we the real followers of Gandhi to enjoy the essence of humanistic religion ?

4

THE SOCIO-CULTURAL ASPECTS OF GANDHIAN HUMANISM

TO EMBRACE everyone as very own and to endear everyone anywhere or everywhere are the essential points of excellence of man as man. He alone knows how to be merged in all so that the very 'I' in him becomes glorified in 'We'. He alone becomes *men* in a man. He eliminates or at least tries to eliminate the littleness in him, for the world of vastness continually beckons him. He averts all avenues of affluence, for the joy of nothingness brings forth serenity and poignance.

To be a man of culture is to be social in the sense that there is a promise of a service towards one and all. Bereft of this sense of service towards one and all, man loses the very poignance and serenity of culture. A truly social man cannot sacrifice culture at any cost. Nursled in his Motherland of whose culture and social uniqueness he should always boast, he purifies himself through the lesson of simplicity that poignantly speaks of his social upbringing and culture.

A humanist *par excellence,* Gandhi highlights the socio-cultural aspects of humanism from the point of view of simplicity that he has practised and followed throughout his life. In fact, his very day-to-day life is an unparalleled emblem of simplicity — a symbol of the Indian socio-cultural life. While commenting on the personal behaviour as desired by him, Gandhi wrote on July 17, 1937 in *Harijan* :

> History tells us of Pratap and Shivaji living in the utmost simplicity. But opinion may be divided as to what they did when they had power. There is no division of opinion about the prophet, Abu Bakr and Omar. They had the riches of the world at their feet. It will be difficult to find a historical parallel to match their rigorous life. Omar would not brook the idea of his lieutenants in the distant provinces using

> anything but coarse cloth and coarse flour.
> . . . It is hardly necessary for me to point out that simplicity does not mean shoddiness. There is a beauty and an art in simplicity which he who runs may see. It does not require money to be neat, clean and dignified. Pomp and pageantry are often synonymous with vulgarity.
>
> — D. G. Tendulkar : *Mahatma*, Publications Division, Ministry of Information and Broadcasting, Government of India, Vol IV, p. 170.

As for cultural poignance, Gandhi believes in the development and enrichment of personality in one's own indigenous brilliance, however meagre it might appeal. The light of one's own land hallowed by socio-cultural richness is the light of true humanism to be allowed to thrive in everyone's approach to life. As Gandhi firmly observes,

> As to the habit of looking to the West for light, I can give little guidance if the whole of my life has not provided any. Light used to go out from the East. If the Eastern reservoir has become empty, naturally the East will have to borrow from the West. I wonder if light, if it is light and not a miasma, can ever be exhausted. As a boy I learnt that it grew with the giving. Anyway I have acted in that belief and have, therefore, traded on the ancestral capital. It has never failed me. This, however, does not mean that I must act like a frog in the well. There is nothing to prevent me from profiting by the light that may come from the West. Only I must take care that I am not overpowered by the glamour of the West. I must not mistake the glamour for true light.
>
> — M. K. Gandhi : *Harijan*, January 13, 1940, p. 414.

Again, while admitting the richness and variety of the Western-culture that is the outcome of finer social appreciation and cohesion, Gandhi ensures that spirit of humanism by means of devotion to appreciation for national tradition and culture. The devotion thus adhered to contributes a lot to the enrichment of socialistic viewpoints as well, which in the end turns out to be one's endearing religion. Referring to this spirit of socio-cultural consciousness, Gandhi remarks :

> Nothing can be farther from my thought that we should become exclusive or erect barriers. But I do respectfully, contend that an appreciation of other cultures can fitly follow, never precede, an appreciation and assimilation of our own. It is my firm opinion that no culture has treasures so rich as ours has. We have not known it. We have been made even to deprecate its study and depreciate its value. We have almost ceased to live it. An academic grasp without practice behind it is like an enbalmed corpse, perhaps lovely too look at but nothing to inspire or ennoble. My religion forbids me to be little or disregard other cultures, as it insists under pain of civil suicide upon imbibing and living my own.
>
> — M. K. Gandhi : *Young India,* September, 1, 1921, p. 276.

To synthesise culture with humanism, Gandhi makes a broad-based view of culture as a global point of unison. The exercise of individual freedom with an eye to enrich one's culture ennobles the blending of global culture with the spirit of humanism. For this lesson of blending, we need not require to follow the footprints of others. Our own ancestral heritage of culture is enough to teach with its great richness and grand varieties. Let us have the Gandhian reminder :

> Many of us are striving to produce a blend of all the cultures which seem today to be in clash with one another. No culture can live, if it attempts to be exclusive. There is no such thing as pure Aryan culture in existence today in India. Whether the Aryans were indigenous to India or were unwelcome intruders, does not interest me much. What does interest me is the fact that my remote ancestors blended with one another with the utmost freedom and we of the present generation are a result of that blend. Whether we are doing any good to the country of our birth and the tiny globe which sustains us or whether we are burden, the future alone will show.
>
> — M. K.Gandhi, *Harijan,* May 9, 1936, p. 100.

To be christened with the true spirit of humanism is to be aware of the age-long social customs and tradition and the cultural progress of mankind. Gandhi gives primary importance to the blending of ancient and modern culture 'based on the traditions of the past and enriched by the experience of later times'. Then, and then only, there can be an ideal social and cultural synthesis in a country that fosters humanism. As a progressive thinker of humanism and culture, he emphasises more on the harmony of social and cultural norms than on anything else so that sanity of humanity does not remain unheeded by mankind. This is evident in his spelling out the objectives of the dissemination of culture as referred to by him in the ideals of the Gujarat Vidyapith :

> It rather hopes to build a new culture based on the traditions of the past and enriched by the experience of later times. It stands for synthesis of the different cultures that have come to stay in India, that have influenced Indian life, and that, in their turn, have themselves been influenced by the spirit of the soil. The synthesis will naturally be of the *Swadeshi* type, where each culture is assured its legitimate place, and not of the American pattern, when one dominant culture absorbs the rest, and where the aim is not towards harmony, but towards an artificial and forced unity.
>
> — M. K. Gandhi : *Young India,* November 17, 1920.

Rather biased in indigenous culture and tradition Gandhi squeezes his pattern and aims of culture at times but that does not necessarily mean that he is averse to the American or any other foreign culture. Nor does he want to belittle the culture of the West, for he never desires to be walled by narrow domestic culture and tradition of his own country. As a great cultural and humanistic visionary, he frankly admits :

> I do not want my house to be walled in on all sides and my window to be stuffed. I want the culture of all lands to be blown about my house as freely as possible.
> . . . Mine is not a religion of the prison-house.
>
> — M. K. Gandhi : *Young India,* June 1, 1921, p. 170.

With the above role of a great visionary, Gandhi seeks

emancipation of mankind by means of service to one and all — a unification of mankind through self-purification in the service of the society . His mission is one of dedication to humanity to this effect. As he observes,

> My work will be finished if I succeed in carrying conviction to the human family, that every man or woman however weak in body, is the guardian of his or her self-respect and liberty. This defence avails, though the whole world may be against the individual resister.
>
> — *The Hindusthan Standard,* Calcutta, August 6, 1944.

To uphold individual dignity in the society for desirable and better advancement of humanism is what Gandhi considers to be of significant importance. For this, every man in the society must be provided with ample freedom to exercise his own incomparable creative and critical consciousness for the well-being of the human society. As a humanist, Gandhi, therefore, gives primary importance to social service than to politics. As he frankly observes,

> My work of social reforms was in no way less or subordinate to political work. . . . I took to the latter and only to the extent that it helped the former. I must therefore confess that work of social reform or self-purification of this manner is a hundred times dearer to me than what is called purely political work.
>
> — M. K. Gandhi : *Young India,* August 6, 1931, p. 203.

With the vision of a social thinker as above, Gandhi elucidates his socio-cultural viewpoints of humanism from a broadbased angle of nationalism. Freedom of the country as he thinks, is freedom of the world. This also enhances the spirit of nationalism as a socio-cultural awakening in humanism. A liberal attitude to the freedom for global awakening by a synthesis of intersocial and inter-cultural heritage of ideals as set forth by him paves a new dimension to humanism :

> I do not want the freedom of India if it means the extinction of England or the disappearance of Englishmen. I want the freedom of my country so that other countries may learn

> something from my free country, so that the resources of my country might be utilised for the benefits of mankind. Just as the cult of patriotism teaches us today that the individual has to die for the family, the family has to die for the village, the village for the district, the district for the province, and province for the country. Even so, a country has to free in order that it may die, if necessary, for the benefit of the world. My idea of nationalism, is that my country may become free, that if need be, the whole country may die, so that the human races may live.
>
> — Mahadev Desai, *Gandhiji in Indian Villages,* Ganesan, Triplicane, Madras, 1927, p. 170.

The sense of neighbourliness and sympathy born of mutual social and cultural exchange and interdependence as Gandhi believes, widens the spectrum of humanism. Unless mankind is aware of this invaluable sense the idea of treating the world as one Big Society of Mankind becomes meaningless and a myth. Side-by-side with self-sufficiency, what is of genuine importance for the march of human society is interdependence. Gandhi, therefore, widens the concept of self-sufficiency from the socio-cultural points of view :

> Interdependence is and ought to be as much the ideal of man as self-sufficiency. Man is a social being. Without interrelation with society he cannot realise his oneness with the universe or suppress his egotism. His social interdependence enables him to test his faith and to prove himself on the touchstone of reality. If man were so placed or could so place himself as to be absolutely above all dependence on his fellow beings he would become so proud and arrogant as to be a veritable burden and nuisance to the world. Dependence on society teaches him the lesson of humanity.
>
> — R. K. Prabhu & U. R. Rao (compiled) : *The Mind of Mahatma Gandhi,* Oxford University Press, London 1945, p. 136.

For the sake of social interdependence to bring about cohesion and the true spirit of humanism, Gandhi even goes a revolutionary step forward to sacrifice self-sufficiency, for he greatly fears that it might breed the poisonous germs of isolation of humanity in the society. The socio-cultural bond of humanity might get a several set back due to utter self-activity self-interest and self-sufficiency. Gandhi, therefore, forewarns humanity against the ills of self-sufficiency as an outcome of introducing the spinning wheel. As he observes,

> That a man ought to be able to satisfy most of his external needs himself is obvious; but it is no less obvious to me that when self-sufficiency is carried to the length of isolating oneself from society it almost amounts to sin. A man cannot become self-sufficient even in respect of all the various operations from the growing of cotton to the spinning of the yarn. He has at some stage or other to take the aid of the members of his family. And if one may take the help from one's own family, why not from one's neighbours ? or otherwise what is the significance of the great saying, 'The world is my family' ?
>
> —*Ibid.*

To actualise the truth of the saying that the world is a big society or family of our very own, Gandhi emphasises on self-purification as the primary objective of mankind. Each one of us, as he categorically asserts, must continually strive for enkindling he nobler social values inherent within in dormant forms for the good of mankind. Purity of heart is an essential pre-condition to service to oneself in order to do greater service to humanity. As he characteristically points out,

> One cannot do good to the country by injuring himself or his family. Similarly one cannot serve the country injuring the world at large. In the final analysis, we must die that the family may live, the family must die that the country may live and the country must die that the world may live. But only pure things can be offered in sacrifice. Therefore, self-purification is the first step. When the heart is pure, we at once realise what is our duty at every moment.
>
> — Mahadev Desai : *The Diary of Mahadev Desai*, Navajivan Publishing House, Ahmedabad 1953, p. 287.

As a social revolutionary, Gandhi wants to point out of the essential needs of the synthesis of minds the crucial avenues of excellence of equality — the fundamental equality of man. He, therefore, thinks it appropriate to wage an endless war against the forces that deprive one of the fruits of one's labour. A socio-cultural synthesis is, as he rightly observes, possible only when the imbalance of the haves and the have-nots are eliminated by means of non-co-operation with inequality and injustice:

> Every man has an equal right to the necessaries of life even as birds and beasts have. And since every right carries with it a corresponding duty and the corresponding remedy for resisting any attack upon it, it is merely a matter of finding out the corresponding duties and remedies to vindicate the elementary fundamental equality. The corresponding duty is to labour with my limbs and the corresponding remedy is to non-co-operate with him who deprives me of the fruit of my labour. And if I would recognise the fundamental equality, as I must, of the capitalist and the labourer, I must strive for his conversion. My non-co-operation with him will open his eyes to the wrong he may be doing.
>
> — R. K. Prabhu & U. R. Rao (compiled) : *The Mind of Mahatma Gandhi*, Oxford University Press, London, 1945, p. 116.

As a matter of fact, social exploitation as Gandhi believes, can only be eliminated when the exploited poor are taught to non-co-operate with the exploiter. This social consciousness is a consciousness of culture within — a consciousness that reminds one of the invaluable dignity of man as a social being. As he opens a newer avenue of thinking on capitalism and exploitation moulded in the socio-cultural aspect of human sensibilities,

> Exploitation of the poor can be extinguished not by effecting the destruction of a few millionaires, but by removing the ignorance of the poor and teaching them to non-co-operate with the exploiters. That will convert the exploiters also. I have even suggested that it will ultimately lead to both being equal partners. Capital as such is not evil; it is its wrong use

> that is evil. Capital in some form or other will always be needed.
>
> — Mahatma Gandhi : *Harijan*, July 28, 1940, p. 219.

To avert inferiority complex arising out of cornered and vested capitalism in the society is, as Gandhi thinks, to maintain, at any cost, the dignity of labour, which must not be pawned to capitalism. In fact, to avert complexities and chaos is not to allow criss-cross of capitalism and labour, but to find out the essential points of harmony between the two. As Gandhi suggests,

> Moneyed men after all form a microscopic minority in the world. They will act on the square. To inflame labour against moneyed man is to perpetuate class hatred and all the evil consequences flowing from it. The strife is a vicious circle to be avoided at any cost. It is an admission of weakness, a sign of inferiority complex. The moment labour recognises its own dignity, money will find its rightful place, i.e. it will be held in trust for labour. For labour is more than money.
>
> — M. K. Gandhi : *Harijan*, October 16, 1945, p. 285.

By the way, Gandhi voices his protest against the centralisation of the necessaries of life as the objectives towards socio-cultured humanism. He also protests against opening of the western approach to socialisation through rapid industrialisation that will bring forth national disaster. Promotion of village crafts and adherence to non-violence are the essential points of advancement that contribute a lot to social and cultural heritage of which we can certainly boast. In his own words,

> If I can convert the country to my point of view, the social order of the future will be based predominantly on the charkha and all it implies. It will include everything that promotes the well-being of the villagers. I do visualise electricity, shipbuilding, iron-works, machine-making and the like existing side-by-side with village handicrafts. But the order of dependence will be reversed. Hitherto the industrialisation has been so planned as to destroy the villages and village

> crafts. In the state of the future, it will subserve the villages and their crafts. I do not believe the socialist belief that the centralisation of the necessaries of life will conduce to the common welfare, when the centralised industries are planned and owned by the state. The socialistic conception of the West was born in an environment reeking with violence. The motive lying behind the western and eastern type is the same — the greatest welfare of the whole society and the abolition of the hideous inequalities resulting in the existence of millions of have-nots and a handful of haves. I believe that this can be achieved only when non-violence is accepted by the best mind of the world as the basis on which a just social order is to be constructed. I hold that the coming into power of the proletariat through violence. . . must be lost before superior violence.
>
> — D. G. Tendulkar : *Mahatma,* Publications Division, Ministry of Information and Broadcasting, Government of India, Vol. V, p. 225.

For a real social renaissance, Gandhi believes in the change of attitude of people through humanistic enterprise in the society. When he wants to introduce the spinning wheel, he considers it to be a means to an end — socio-cultural excellence — and never an end in itself. For a permanent change of attitude an adherence to persuasiveness coupled with tolerance as a social transformer is not only necessary but also mandatory. The assurance of social progress is primarily dependent on a keen and lasting interest and attention to any social endeavour. As a practical visionary, Gandhi distinctly observes,

> Our contact with them (the villagers) begins with their service through the spinning wheel, but it does not end there. The spinning wheel is the centre of that service. If you spend your next vacation in some far off village in the interior you will see the truth of my remark. You will find the people cheerless and fear-stricken. You will find houses in ruins. You will look in vain for any sanitary hygienic conditions. You will find the cattle in a miserable way, and yet you will see idleness stalking there. The people will tell you of the spinning wheel having been in their homes long ago, but today they will entertain no talk of it or of any other cottage industry.

> They have no hope left in them. They live, for they cannot die at will. They will spin only if *you* spin. Even if a hundred out of a population of 300 in a village spin, you assure them of an additional income of Rs. 1,800 a year. You can lay the foundation of solid reform on this income in every village. It is easy I know to say this, but difficult to do. Faith can make it easy. 'I am alone, how can I reach seven hundred thousand villages?' — This is the argument that pride whispers to us. Start with the faith that if you fix yourself up in one single village and succeed, the rest will follow. Progress is then assured.
>
> — M. K. Gandhi : *Young India*, June 17, 1926, p. 217.

Any constructive programme to bring about the least socio-cultural change necessitates, as Gandhi rightly thinks, modesty and persuasiveness in approach. Education takes a major role to reorient both socially and individually, the true humanistic spirit in an individual. It also enables to bridge the gulf between the haves and the have-nots. In fact, the extinction of socio-cultural disparities is possible only when education launches a revolution in the poorer sections of the society. As Gandhi elucidates,

> The *Kisan* or the peasant, whether as a landless labourer or a labouring proprietor, comes first. He is the salt of the earth which rightly belongs or should belong to him, not to the absentee landlord or zamindar. But in the non-violent way the labourer cannot forcibly eject the absentee landlord. He has so to work as to make it impossible for the landlord to exploit him. Closest co-operation among the peasants is absolutely necessary. To this end special organising bodies or committees should be formed where there are none and those already in existence should be reformed where necessary. The *Kisans* are for the most part illiterate. Both adults and young persons of school-going age should be educated. This applies to men and women. When they are landless labourers their wages should be brought to a level that would ensure a decent living which should mean balanced food, dwelling houses and clothing, which should satisfy health requirements.
>
> — *The Hindusthan Standard*, October, 1944.

To launch any constructive work for social change by means of spelling out well-defined objectives in terms of humanistic enterprise is to go ahead for true and practical humanism. For a practical revolution in social humanism, Gandhi makes a radical point of departure from the concept of women normally denounced as mere partners to sexual purposes and inclinations. He places women as a forerunner of socio-cultural evolution and considers them to be ideal disseminators of truth and non-violence. As a matter of fact, he shows new dimensions of the role of women in the advancement of humanism as socio-cultural exponents in this bizarre world of ours caged in timelessness :

> In my opinion, it is degrading both for man and woman that woman should be called upon or induced to forsake the hearth and shoulder the rifle for the protection of that hearth. It is a reversion to barbarity and the beginning of the end. In trying to ride the horse that man rides, she brings herself and him down. The sin will be on the man's head for tempting or compelling his companion to desert her special calling. There is as much bravery in keeping one's home in good order and condition, as there is in defending it against attack from without.
>
> As I have watched millions of peasants in their natural surroundings and as I watch them daily in little Segaon, the natural division of spheres of work has forced itself on my attention. There are no women blacksmiths and no women carpenters. But men and women work on the fields, the heaviest work being done by the males. The women keep and manage the homes. They supplement the meagre resources of the family, but man remains the main bread-winner. The vision of the spheres of work being recognised, the general qualities and culture required are practically the same for both the sexes.
>
> My contribution to the great problem lies in my presenting for acceptance truth and ahimsa in every walk of life, whether for the individuals or nations. I have hugged the hope that in this the woman will be the unquestioned leader and, having thus found her place in human evolution, will shed her inferiority complex. If she is able to do this successfully, she must resolutely refuse to believe in the

> modern teaching that everything is determined and regulated by the sex impulse. I do not know that the millions of men who are taking an active part in the war are obsessed by the sex spectre. Nor are the peasants working together in their fields worried or dominated by it. This is not to say or suggest that they are free from the instinct implanted in man and woman. But it must certainly does not dominate their lives as it seems to dominate the lives of those who are saturated with the modern sex literature. Neither man nor woman has time for such things, when he or she is faced with the hard fact of living life in its grim reality,...
>
> — D. G. Tendulkar : *Mahatma*, Publications Division, Ministry of Information and Broadcasting, Government of India, Vol. V, p. 227.

As a socio-cultural exponent of humanism, Gandhi glorifies the role of women in terms of *ahimsa*, for he thinks that women alone teach the lesson of tolerance in the society by undergoing mute suffering. He, therefore, pays great importance to women for their love and affection that teach humanity how to negotiate the ills of the society in day-to-day life. As a 'silent leader' a woman knows, as Gandhi believes, how to orient humanity from socio-cultural points of view. As he poignantly observes,

> Woman is the incarnation of ahimsa. *Ahimsa* means infinite love, which again means infinite capacity for suffering. And who but woman, the mother of man, shows this capacity in the largest measure ? She knows it as she carries the infant and feeds it during nine months and she derives joy in the suffering involved. What can beat the suffering caused by the pangs of labour ? But she forgets them in the joy of creation. Who again suffers daily, so that her babe may wax from day-to-day ? Let her translate that love to the whole of humanity, let her forget that she ever was or can be the object of man's lust. And she will occupy her proud position by the side of man as his mother, maker and silent leader. It is given to her to teach the art of peace to the warring world thirsting for that nectar. She can become the leader in satyagraha which does not require the learning that the books give but does

> require the stout heart that comes from suffering and faith.
>
> — *Ibid.*, pp. 227-228.

The social antagonisms standing in the way of union of minds between man and woman also aches the heart of Gandhi who considers the tragic eventualities between a man and his partner by any reason whatsoever as a socio-cultural failure. The ills of 'social ostracism' — the ills that even now invite fundamentalism, communalism, hatred and violence in the society — necessitate a re-evaluation in terms of Gandhian humanism. Elucidating the liberty of young men and women to take any decision of their marriages in any form, whatsoever and howsoever, Gandhi asserts :

> Marriage taboos are not universal and are largely based on social usage. The usage varies from province to province and as between different divisions. This does not mean that the youth may ride rough-shod over all established social customs and inhibitions. Before they decided to do so, they must convert public opinion to their side. In the meantime, the individuals concerned ought patiently to bide their time, or if they cannot do that calmly and quietly to face the consequences of social ostracism.
>
> At the same time, it is equally the duty of society not to take up a heartless stepmotherly attitude towards those who might disregard or break the established conventions.
>
> — M. K. Gandhi : *Harijan*, May 29, 1937, p. 125.

Gandhi's own upbringing as a social humanist has freed himself from any type of hatred and exploitation. A cultural human consciousness in him has always elevated him towards finer visions of life in self-discipline and humility. His frank statement clarifies the point :

> I hold myself to be incapable of hating any being on earth. By a long course of prayerful discipline, I have ceased for over forty years to hate anybody. I know this is a big claim. Nevertheless, I make it in all humility. But I can and do hate evil wherever it exists. I hate the system of government that the British people have

> set up in India. I hate the ruthless exploitation of India even as I hate from the bottom of my heart the hideous system of untouchability for which millions of Hindus have made themselves responsible. But I do not hate the domineering Englishmen as I refuse to hate the domineering Hindus. I seek to reform them in all the loving ways that are open to me. My non-co-operation has its roots not in hatred but in love.
>
> — M. K. Gandhi : *Young India,* August 6, 1925, p. 272.

To be deeply integrated with the social structure is not only to eliminate class hatred but also to be inspired with the zeal for furtherance of humanism. Gandhi, therefore, calls upon the sense of dedication for service towards mankind as an essential symbol of culture. Admittedly, his theory of trusteeship is christened with the spirit of broader socio-cultural humanism. Speaking about the role of princes, he remarks :

> For my part I desire not abolition, but conversion of their autocracy into trusteeship, not in name but in reality. The arbitrary powers they enjoy should go. The liberty of the people should not depend upon the will of an individual however noble and ancient may be his descent. Nor can any person, whether prince or a princely zamindar or merchant, be the sole owner and disposer of possessions hereditary or self-acquired. Every individual must have the fullest liberty to use his talents consistently with equal use by his neighbours but no one is entitled to the arbitrary use of the gains from the talents. He is part of the nation or say the social structure surrounding him. Therefore he can only use his talents not for self only but for the social structure of which he is but a part and on whose sufferance he lives.
>
> — M. K. Gandhi : *Harijan*, August 2, 1942, p. 249.

Like a celebrated socio-cultural visionary, Gandhi highlights on self-understanding and appeals to self-conscience to usher forth a worthier era of socio-cultural transcendence by dissociation of inequalities. As he remarks,

> The present inequalities are surely due to people's ignorance. With a growing knowledge of their natural strength, the inequalities must disappear. If the revolution is brought about by violence the position will be reversed, but not altered for the better. With non-violence, i.e., conversion, the new era which people hope for must be born. My approach and appeal are in terms of non-violence pure and undefiled. The French have a noble motto in Liberty, Equality, Fraternity. It is a heritage not for the French only but for all mankind.
>
> — M.K. Gandhi : *Harijan, Ibid.*

The nurturing of fearlessness to confront violence is, as Gandhi rightly feels, the prime need of humanism. A new culture — a culture of looking within amid a new spirit of askance and adventure — is sure to beckon greater prospects of socio-cultural upbringing of humanity. In his own words.

> The remedy against cowardice is not physical culture but the braving of dangers. So long as parents of the middle-class Hindus, themselves timid, continue to transmit their timidity by keeping their grown-up children in cotton-wool, so long will there be the desire to shun dangers and run no risks. They will have to dare to leave their children alone, let them run risks and even at times get killed in so doing. The puniest individual may have a stout heart.
>
> — M. K. Gandhi : *Young India,* May 29, 1924, p. 177.

Side-by-side with the culture of fearlessness for true humanism, Gandhi advocates for the cleanliness of the mind and body — a very essential component to be attuned to social harmony and cultural excellence. This is an education which is even now lacking in the socialisation of mankind. As he explains,

> Cleanliness of the mind and body is the first step in education. Prayer does for the purification of the mind, what the bucket and the broom do for the cleaning up our physical surroundings. And that is why we always commence our proceedings with prayer. No matter whether the prayer we

> recite is the Hindu prayer or the Muslim or the Parsi, its function is essentially the same, namely, purification of the heart. God has innumerable names but the most beautiful and suitable, in my opinion, is Truth. Let Truth, therefore, rule every action of our life, be it ever so insignificant. Let every morsel of good that we eat be sanctified with His name and not only will it make our bodies and minds healthy and clean, the inner cleanliness will be reflected in our surroundings also. We must learn to make our latrine as clean as our kitchens.
>
> As with the individual, so with the society. A village is but a group of individuals, and the world, as I see it, is one vast village, and mankind one family. The various functions in the human body have been parallel in the corporate life of society. What I have said about inner and outer cleanliness of the individual, therefore, applies to the whole society.
>
> — D. G. Tendulkar : *Mahatma,* Publications Division, Ministry of Information and Broadcasting, Government of India, Vol. VI, pp. 297-298.

The real test of socialism, and for that end in view, culture and humanism, starts with the inner process of greatness of humanity. This greatness is the greatness of self-purification in order to be of utmost use to the society. Individual excellence is, therefore, the excellence for preparing oneself continually to the service of society and humanity. Self-purification starts when Truth is allowed to be enkindled within oneself. Gandhi considers it to be an ardent task to be christened with *atmavat sarvabhutesu* — the spirit of looking upon everyone as one's very own. A world of people sharing and enjoying a communicated experience of life and work enhances the spirit of social synchronisation and culture. The progress of humanism and culture is basically dependent on how an individual merges in the society for the common good of one and all. Gandhi's philosophy of the *Swaraj* is based on the Truth of goodness for everyone. As he observes :

> The *Swaraj* of my dream recognises no race or religious distinction. Nor is it to be the monopoly of the latter persons nor yet of moneyed men. *Swaraj* is to be for all, including the former, but emphatically including the maimed, the blind, the

> starving, toiling millions.
>
> — M. K. Gandhi : *Young India*, September 3, 1925, p. 303.

Again, he remarks :

> The *Swaraj* of my dream is the poor man's *Swaraj*. The necessaries of life should be enjoyed by you in common with those enjoyed by the princes and the moneyed men. But that does not mean that you should have palaces like theirs. They are not necessary for happiness. You or I would be lost in them. But, you ought to get all ordinary amenities of life that a rich man enjoys. I have not the slightest doubt that Swaraj is not *Purna* Swaraj until these amenities are guaranteed to undeı it.
>
> — M. K. Gandhi : *Young India*, March 26, 1931, p. 46.

To live nobly is to learn the art of simplicity and grace of life. A groaning world as ours is, requires simplicity in life through social co-operation and cultural cohesion. Mere industrialisation — a craze of the affluent West — is no answer to the hungry heart craving for peace and grace of life. The culture of plain living is the culture of humanism or transcendence of excellence of finer sensibilities from man to man, from society to society and from country to country. Gandhi calls for the beckoning of that kind of socio-cultural humanism:

> I don't believe that industrialization is necessary in any case for any country. It is much less so for India. Indeed, I believe that independent India can only discharge her duty towards a groaning world by adopting a simple but ennobled life by developing her thousands of cottages and living at peace with the world. High thinking is inconsistent with complicated material life based on high speed imposed on us by Mammon worship. All the grace of life are possible only when we learn the art of living nobly.
>
> There may be sensation in living dangerously. We must draw the distinction between living in the face of danger and living dangerously. A man who dares to live alone in a forest

infested by wild beasts and wilder men without a gun and with God as his only help, lives in the face of danger. A man who lives perpetually in mid-air and dives to the earth below to the admiration of a gaping world, lives dangerously. One is a purposeful, the other a purposeless life.

Whether such plain living is possible for an isolated nation, however large geographically and numerically, in the face of a world armed to the teeth and in the midst of pomp and circumstance, is a question open to the doubt of a sceptic. The answer is straight and simple.

If plain life is worth living, then the attempt is worth making even though only an individual or a group makes the effort.

At the same time I believe that some key industries are necessary. I do not believe in arm-chair or armed socialism. I believe in action according to my belief, without waiting for wholesale conversion. Hence, without having to enumerate the key industries, I would have the state ownership where a large number of people have to work together. The ownership of the products of their labour, whether skilled or unskilled, will vest in them through the state. But as I can conceive such a state only based on non-violence, I would not dispossess monied men by force, but I would invite their co-operation in the process of conversion to state ownership.

* * * *

And I allow this belief in the face of inhumanities we have witnessed and may still have to witness in India as elsewhere. Let us live in the face of danger.

— D. G. Tendulkar : *Mahaṭma*, Publications Division, Ministry of Information and Broadcasting, Government of India, Vol. II, p. 188.

A model of activism in our culture as Gandhi is, his synthesis of global socialism and culture based on restraint by means of adopting non-violenece and interpreting the spirit of the *Gita* in his own unique way in the social and cultural affairs of life and activities have dawned forth a new era of promise and poignance for the world of today and tomorrow.

In fact, he remodels his theory of non-violence by incorporating the spirit of the Indian classics in order to equip it with a poignant rationale of culture. And when he launches his non-violence for socio-cultural regeneration, it has its circumference not limited to nationalistic enterprise alone, but it is always broadbased on the mission of global culture and global society :

> In preparing the central thesis for social change, Gandhi has thus drawn from the total global environs as well as from the culture of restraint and fearlessness embodied by many peoples of the world this knowledge of western society and of the impact of its many exploitative institutions was formidable. He could thus learn of the objectives of probable new world from the contours of the existing one itself.
>
> He got acquainted with the new values right from the days of his self-preparation, from his readings of Ruskin, Thoreau, and Tolstoy. As the got confirmed in his attitude towards vegetarianism in England and as he practised Satyagraha, then called passive resistance, for the first time in South Africa in the set-up of a non-Indian culture, Gandhi developed the constructs of a new theory. Gandhi had also drawn profusely from Christianity, from his knowledge of law and faith in constitutionalism as well as from the negative aspects of imperialism and capitalism. With all these lessons when Gandhi set out to prepare the contours of a new society, what could we have called that mission but a phenomenon of global significance ? Gandhi had, of course, learnt from his indigenous culture as well. But, here again, Gandhi drew more from confrontations he had with the contemporary folk culture of his country and the struggles that his people waged under his own leadership.
>
> * * * *
>
> Gandhi had thus drawn from the total global environment and used that knowledge to build the constructs of a new Indian culture. Accordingly, he also helped to reinterpret some of our own classics, such as the *Gita*, and tried to provide a new rationale for the theory of non-violence,

here on our own soil, in India.

— Sugata Das Gupta : "Truth and Non-violence in Gandhi's Humanism": A symposium paper quoted from *Truth and Non-violence,* edited by T.K. Mahadevan, Gandhi Peace Foundation, New Delhi on behalf of Indian National Commission for co-operation with UNESCO, New Delhi-1, 1970, pp. 343-344.

The confused path of world civilisation today undeniably necessitates a re-orientation through the socio-cultural aspects of Gandhian humanism. In a bruised world the deeper truths of humanity are to be revived in order to avert the impending peril. The essence of humanism lost is never the lost humanism. Somewhere in the corner of the sordid heart of everyone of us rings the Gandhian song of the glory of humanism.

Do we really pay attention to that inherent song ?

5

SARVODAYA AND GANDHIAN HUMANISM

To do good to humanity is the greatest form of the worship of the Almighty. It is to evaluate the worth of oneself as a servant of the All Beautiful. The great truth of mankind is always an outcome of magnanimity and benevolence. It is to eliminate the lower passions and aspirations of human sensibilities and ignite the higher and nobler ones to become a worthy follower of humanism.

How to enkindle the worthier values and norms of life? How to arouse within oneself the spirit of altruism? How to eliminate the evil passions and desires and proclaim the glory of humanism?

An uncompromising crusader against the odds and ills of baser human sensibilities, Gandhi has a broad vision of humanism nurtured in the aura of aesthetic optimism: *Sarve Sukhino bhavantu, sarve santu niramaya* – let every one of us be happy, let all of us be *sans* disease. The disease of mankind – grave and alarming – is continually paving path to erosion of human values and sensibilities. Who ignores that the world is tilting in the balance of decay and destruction ? The God of Truth – *Satyanarayana* – is yet to be visualised by a bruised humanity primarily because the minds of men everywhere in the world are engulfed with the horrible fear of extinction. A sense of insecurity within each individual is a telling sign of dissociation from the belief of God within each one of us. For a great awakening of all within ourselves, let us listen to the poignant words of a great seer:

> We must give up all external fears. But the internal foes we must always fear. We are rightly afraid of animal passion, anger, and the like. External fears cease of their own accord, when once we have conquered these traitors within the camp. All such fears revolve round the body as the centre, and will therefore, disappear as soon

> as one gets rid of attachment for the body. We thus find that all external fear is the baseless fabric of our own vision. Fear has no place in our hearts, when we have shaken off the attachment for wealth, for family and for the body. Nothing whatever in the world is ours. Even we ourselves are His. When we cease to be masters, and reduce ourselves to the rank of servants, humbler than the very dust under our feet, all fears will roll away like mist, we shall attain ineffable peace, and see *Satyanarayana* (The God of Truth) face to face.
>
> – M.K. Gandhi: *From Yeravda Mandir*, Navajivan Press, Ahmedabad, 1935, p. 43.

Endearing mankind rather than nursing hatred towards humanity is the key to Gandhian humanism. The warmth of humanism is, therefore, best felt in awaiting the awakening of good sense. Let all purify themselves with the sense of brotherly affection and love. Let existence with honour and not extinction in hatred and enmity be the end in view of humanism. In his concept of *Sarvodaya*, Gandhi himself proclaims his view on mutual fraternity:

> Having flung aside the sword, there is nothing except the cup of love which I can offer to those who oppose me. It is by offering that cup that I expect to draw them close to me. I cannot think of permanent enmity between man and man and believing as I do in the theory of rebirth, I live in the hope that, if not in this birth, in some other birth, I shall be able to hug all humanity in friendly embrace.
>
> – M.K. Gandhi: *Young India*, April 2, 1931, p. 94.

When Gandhi speaks of *Sarvodaya* as an inherent force for unison of mankind as one great and beautiful creation of God, he emphasises on the omnipresence of the soul anywhere and everywhere. As the soul's movement is endless so the good sense and sensibilities of mankind continually boost humanity towards nobler and higher ends. To ignore this is to betray Truth pure and serne. The humdrum daily affairs of life create a covering that hides this Truth. It is our duty as men and women striving towards perfection, to eliminate littleness and to extend a broadened vision of Truth. Gandhi characteristically elucidates this point:

> It has been truly said, that desire for enjoyment creates bodies for the soul; when this desire vanishes, there remains no further need for the body, and man is freed from the vicious cycle of births and deaths. The soul is omnipresent; why should she care to be confined within the cage-like body or do evil and even kill for the sake of that cage. We thus arrive at the ideal of total renunciation, and learn to use the body for the purposes of service so long as it exists, so much so that service, and not bread, becomes with us the staff of life. We eat and drink, sleep and wake, for service alone. Such an attitude of mind brings us real happiness, and the beatific vision in the fulness of time.
>
> – M.K. Gandhi: *From Yeravda Mandir*, Navajivan Press, Ahmedabad, 1935, p. 37.

The good of one for the good of all and *vice versa* as Gandhi propounds in his *Sarvodaya* is in essence the spirit of humanism recast and remodelled on the great Indian saying: *Vasudhaiva Kutumbakam*. It is also an echo of Ruskin's *Unto This Last* from where Gandhi nursles the humanistic spirit of *Sarvodaya*:

(i) That the good of the individual is contained in the good of all.

(ii) That a lawyer's work has the same value as the barber's in as much as all have the same right of earning their livelihood from their work.

(iii) That a life of labour, i.e. the life of the tiller of the soil and the handicraftsman is the life worth living.

– M.K. Gandhi: *An Autobiography*, Navajivan Publishing House, Ahmedabad, 1940, p. 365.

Gandhi, therefore, thinks that for practical humanism what is badly needed is equalisation of status. This will eliminate undesirable differences between man and man. In his words,

> I want to bring about an equalisation of status. The working classes have all these centuries been isolated and relegated to a lower class. They have been *Shoodras*, and the word has been interpreted to mean an inferior status. I want to allow no differentiation between the son of a weaver, of an agriculturist and of a schoolmaster.
>
> – M.K. Gandhi, *Harijan*, January 15, 1938, p. 416.

As a humanistic visionary, Gandhi hopes for a regeneration of India in the elimination of economic and social disparities. Let the good sense of living together, sharing mutual weal and woe, laughter and tears, and negotiating diverse differences usher forth a new horizon of humanism:

> According to me, the economic constitution of India and for the matter of that of the world, should be such that no one under it should suffer from want of food and clothing. In other words, everybody should be able to get sufficient work to enable him to make the two ends meet. And this ideal can be universally realised only if the means of production of the elementary necessaries of life remain in the control of the masses. These should be freely available to all as God's air and water are or ought to be, they should not be made a vehicle of traffic for the exploitation of others. Their monopolisation by any country, nation or group of persons would be unjust. The neglect of this simple principle is the cause of the destitution that we witness today not only in this unhappy land but in other parts of the world too.
>
> – M.K. Gandhi: *Young India*, November 15, 1928, p. 381

Through his own unparalleled power of introspection, Gandhi knows that it is man who becomes an enemy of man and he, therefore, emphasises on the sensible man, an inherent man born with the spirit of *Sarvodaya* to become worthy of man. The 'grand dream of emancipation of man' as he does, bears a definite stamp of difference from the dream of Ruskin:

> Indeed, Gandhi believed that everybody could do what he had

done. 'You are as strong as you think you are', he would say, 'you are as strong as I am'. This faith in the ordinary man is what illumines the path for us in the future. For his message is to all of us, to each one of us; and its burden is that the common man can yet reassert his humanism if he has faith in his cause.

Gandhi's conception of sarvodaya signifies the welfare and service of all. A good life for all and not just for the majority provides the test. In the society of Gandhi's dreams, the most needy will be provided for and none will be forgotten or allowed to feel lost. 'Unto this last'; even the least will be cared for. This grand dream of the emancipation of man had other facets also.

Ruskin's *Unto this Last*, which Gandhi read in 1904, denounced classical economists for not conceiving economics in terms of human welfare and accused industrialism of being responsible for intensifying poverty and injustice. These ideas found a ready response in Gandhi's mind. The ideal of simple life and the stress on manual work took on their true significance in his quest. He found that though science and technology had given a new turn to the wheel of production and wealth, men were not only not emancipated, but were in fact being exploited. To Gandhi man himself was the cause of his own exploitation, because he had created machines and a huge centralised structure, and thus both in the political and economic fields, man had defeated man. He, therefore, called for a review of the old assumptions and for a reassessment of the scale of values. His emphasis on simplicity and limitation of wants, his stress on decentralisation and participation by the common man in the decision-making process at various levels, his call to men to work with joy, his emphasis on a united but not a uniform world – all this has a current relevance.

– S. Chakravarti: Truth and Non-violence in Gandhi's Humanism', *Truth and Non-violence*, Edited by T.K. Mahadevan, Gandhi Peace Foundation, New Delhi, on behalf of Indian National Commission for Co-operation with UNESCO, 1970, pp. 39-40.

The principle of austerity as one of the outcomes of *Sarvodaya* signifies the worth of humanism. That a man finds his true perspective through simplicity is the basic principle of Gandhian humanism. It serves as a weapon to combat all evil forces. It encourages him to remain firm in his conviction for Truth which is the essence of humanism. One who follows the path of simplicity also becomes patient in one's search for the glory of humanism. While explaining the course of launching non-violence, Gandhi highlights this basic principle of humanity and patience as the symbol of *Sarvodaya*:

> The *satyagrahi*'s course is plain. He must stand unmoved in the midst of all cross-currents. He may not be impatient with blind orthodoxy, nor be irritated over the unbelief of the suppressed people. He must know that his suffering will melt the stoniest heart of the stoniest fanatic and that it will also be a wall of protection for the wavering *panchama* brother who has been held under the suppression for ages. He must know that relief will come when there is least hope for it. For such is the way of the cruelly kind Deity who insists upon testing His devotee through a fiery furnace and delights in humbling him to the dust.
>
> – M.K. Gandhi: *Young India*, June 4, 1925, p. 189.

To live in the spirit of continual inward purity and patience is to live the life of a humanist, and Gandhi goes so for as to make a unison between *Sarvodaya* and *Swaraj* by means of upholding the principles of patience and sacrifice. As Gandhi thinks, the principles and strategies of *Swaraj* will teach a new lesson of *Sarvodaya* – a new art of living in self-sacrifice:

> *Swaraj* won without sacrifice cannot last long. I would therefore like our people to get ready to make the highest sacrifice that they are capable of. In true sacrifice all the suffering is on one side – one is required to master the art of getting killed without killing, of gaining life by losing it.
>
> – M.K. Gandhi: *Young India*, May 8, 1930, p. 161.

Side by side with the art of self-sacrifice as one of the outcomes of *Sarvodaya*, the practice of self-control as Gandhi feels and acts accordingly, is also essential, for the practice of self-control is the practice of purification of the human sensibilities. He, therefore, advises on boosting higher thoughts and nobler feelings as strategies for efflorescence of *Sarvodaya*:

> Everyone must remember that his most secret thoughts have an influence on himself as well as on others. He should, therefore, practise self-control, so as to put all evil thoughts out of his mind, and give room only for thoughts that are noble and great. He should keep his body as clean and spotless as his mind.
>
> – M.K. Gandhi: *Ethical Religion*, S. Ganesan, Triplicane, Madras, 1930, p. 59.

The education of earnestness and love born out of self-control which one receives through *Sarvodaya*, teaches one how to be modest and how to inculcate the spirit of modesty – *Vinaya* – within oneself under diverse situations. On more than one occasion, Gandhi preaches the message of love which is in fact the message of *Sarvodaya*.

In 1938, while he was in his frontier tour, Gandhi referred to the inherent spirit of love which is the spirit of *Sarvodaya*:

> Man's nature is not essentially evil; brave nature has been known to yield to the influence of love. You must never despair of human nature. . . Don't leave out of your traffic that noblest and most precious of merchandise, love. Give to the tribesmen all the love that you are capable of and you will have theirs in return.
>
> – D.G. Tendulkar: *Mahatma*, Publications Division, Ministry of Information and Broadcasting, Government of India, Vol. IV, p. 296.

The love that preaches the Gandhian philosophy of *Sarvodaya* is, again, the guiding force of the spirit of practical humanism. It aims at harmonisation of humanity by discarding all petty disparities. One recalls how Gandhi preaches the message of love that knows no discord or suffering, to a 30,000 strong crowd who attended the meeting on 8 November, 1933:

> I would like to state in all humility, but with perfect confidence,

> that I have taken up this movement in no spirit of antagonism to any other religion or humanity. It would be impossible to point to any act of mine during the past fifty years which could be proved to have been antagonistic to any person or community. I have never believed anyone to be my enemy. My faith demands that I should consider no one as such. I may not wish ill to anything that lives. It is my firm conviction that if the Hindu heart is completely purged of the taint of untouchability, the event will have its inevitable influence not only upon all the communities in India but also on the whole world. The belief is daily becoming stronger. I cannot remove from my heart untouchability regarding several millions of human beings and harbour it towards some other millions.
>
> – D.G. Tendulkar, *Mahatma*, Publications Division, Ministry of Information and Broadcasting, Government of India, Vol. III, p. 220.

Justifying the reason for removing the ills of untouchability, Gandhi refers to the inseparable relationship between man and God as the great essence of humanism:

> If we believe that we are all children of one and the same God, and God is Truth and Justice, how can there be untouchability amongst us, His children ? God of Truth and Justice can never create distinction of high and low among His own children.
>
> – *Ibid.*, p. 221.

For a life dedicated to the cause of true humanism, the sense of altruism – of doing and thinking for all and reducing oneself to a cipher – is the key-point of Gandhian *Sarvodaya*. For this, Gandhi rightly thinks that everyone of us necessitates a vigorous orientation of conduct in self-sacrifice and self-restraint. This is what he actually means by *brahmacharya*. As he categorically remarks,

> Without overcoming lust man cannot hope to rule over self. And without rule over self there can be no *Swaraj* or *Rama Raj*. Rule of all without rule of oneself would prove to be as deceptive and disappointing as a painted toy-mango, charming to look at

> outwardly but hollow and empty within. No worker who has not overcome lust can hope to render any genuine service to the cause of Harijans, communal unity, *Khadi*, cow protection or village reconstruction. Great causes like these cannot be served by intellectual equipment alone, they call far spiritual effort or soul-force. Soul-force comes only through God's grace, and God's grace never descends upon a man who is a slave to lust.
>
> – M.K. Gandhi: *Harijan*, November 21, 1936, p. 321.

When the question of morality is attained to the efflorescence of humanism, one cannot but avert the consequences of being indifferent to one's actions because the excellence of man is the excellence of individuality that again signifies the essence of *Sarvodaya*, the endeavour for the excellence of all. As moral restraint it generally required for the goodness and welfare of the individual and the society, any deviation from this means that one forsakes the inherent spirit of *Sarvodaya*, Gandhi, therefore, insists upon guarding oneself from animal passions from time to time. As he observes,

> It is good for a person who over-eats to have an ache and a fast. It is bad for him to indulge his appetite and then escape the consequences by taking tonics or other medicine. It is still worse for a person to indulge in his animal passions and escape the consequences of his acts. Nature is relentless and will have full revenge for any such violation of her laws. Moral results can only be produced by moral restraints. All other restraints defeat the very purpose for which they are intended.
>
> – R.K. Prabhu & U.R. Rao (compiled): *The Mind of Mahatma Gandhi*, Oxford University Press, London 1945, p. 108.

As a great follower of the principles of *Sarvodaya*, Gandhi highlights *brahmacharya* not because it is a bare strategy for self-restraint but primarily because it leads the mind towards the goal of humanism. As he introspectively visualises, the excellence of the mind leads to the excellence of the body. Hence *Brahmacharya*:

> *Brahmacharya* must be observed in thought, word and deed. It

may be harmful to suppress the body, if the mind is at the same time allowed to go astray. Where the mind wanders, the body must follow sooner or later.

It is necessary here to appreciate a distinction. It is one thing to allow the mind to harbour impure thoughts; it is a different thing altogether if it strays among them in spite of ourselves. Victory will be ours in the end, if we non-cooperate with the mind in its evil wanderings.

We experience every moment of our lives, that often while the body is subject to our control, the mind is not. This physical control should never be relaxed, and in addition we must put forth a constant endeavour to bring the mind under control. We can do nothing more, nothing less.

– M.K. Gandhi: From *Yeravda Mandir*, Navajivan Press, Ahmedabad, 1935, p. 18.

To control the mind in the Gandhian perspective of *Sarvodaya* is to control one's activities in freedom. A *Sarvodaya* worker, therefore, exercises his freedom of thought uninterruptedly because whenever he works, he works with dedication to the cause of humanism:

As a worker he carries no rights but does carry all the duties attached to that title. In the performance of those duties, he may seek co-operation of any good man, no matter what party ideology he may belong to. But one thing he may never do, he may not abandon truth and non-violence; for, verity, it is the nectar of the *Sarvodaya* ocean.

– Durga Das: *India: From Curzon to Nehru and After*, Rupa & Co., Calcutta, 1977, p. 53.

The aims and objectives, basic principles and programmes of *Sarvodaya* as clearly spelt out by Gandhi are pointers to acceleration of humanistic spirit within mankind. It is also interesting to note that in *Sarvodaya*, Gandhi wants to re-orient the society as a great platform for all-round consciousness for humanism. When Vinoba explains, as follows, the concept of the *Sarvodaya Samaj* and indicates the programme of activities, his vision as a true humanist is evident in practice:

> Those who believe in Mahatma Gandhi's ideology decide to form themselves into a brotherhood.
>
> Name– *Sarvodaya Samaj*
> (*Sarvodaya* means the "Welfare of all" : *Samaj* is "Brotherhood").
>
> Aim – to strive towards a society based on Truth and Non-violence in which there will be no distinctions of class or creed, no opportunity for exploitation and full scope for the development of both individuals as well as groups.
>
> Basic Principle – Instance on the purity of the means as that of the end.
>
> Programme – For the achievement of the aim, the following programme is to be worked:
>
> 1. Communal harmony (friendship between followers of different faiths and sects.)
> 2. Abolition of class distinctions.
> 3. Prohibition.
> 4. Promotion of cottage industries.
> 5. Village sanitation.
> 6. Basic Education.
> 7. Equality of status and rights for both men and women.
> 8. Health and cleanliness.
> 9. Economic Equality.
> 10. Development of agriculture.
> 11. Organisation of labour.
> 12. Welfare of aboriginals.
> 13. Organisation of students.
> 14. Service of lepers.

15. Relief Work.
16. Naturopathy.
17. Other Similar Activities.

– Vinoba Bhave: *Sarvodaya : Its Principles and Programmes*, Navajivan Publishing House, Ahmedabad, 1951, pp. 63-64.

Admittedly, what Gandhi wants through his principles of *Sarvodaya* is to bring forth a certain sense of awareness for conjoint, communicated, serene and blessed living. Such living surely requires a lifelong preparation for service to mankind by means of self-purification and self-discipline. The law of life, as Gandhi thinks teaches us to share all experiences of all mankind for the greater goodness of humanity. For this greater goodness, again, soul-force ultimately triumphs over all inconsistencies and chaos of life. Gandhi explains the march of *Sarvodaya* in terms of history:

> The fact that there are so many men still alive in the world shows that it is based not on the force of arms but on the force of truth or love. Therefore, the greatest and most unimpeachable evidence of the success of this force is to be found in the fact that, in spite of the wars of the world, it still lives on.
>
> Thousands, indeed, tens of thousands, depend on a very active working of this force. Little quarrels of millions of families in their daily lives disappear before the exercise of this force. Hundreds of nations live in peace. History does not and cannot make note of this fact. History is really a record of every interruption of the even working of the force of love or of the soul. Two brothers quarrel; one of them repents and re-awakens the love that was lying dormant in him; the two again begin to live in peace; nobody takes note of this but if the two brothers, through the intervention of solicitors or some other reason take up arms or go to law – which is another form of the exhibition of brute force, – their doings would be immediately noticed in the press, they would be the talk of their neighbours and would probably go down to history. And what is true of families and communities is true of nations. There is no reason to believe that there is one law for families and another for nations. History, then, is a record of an interruption of the course of

nature. Soul-force, being natural, is not noted in history.

> – M.K. Gandhi: *Hind Swaraj or Indian Home Rule*, Navajivan Publishing House, Ahmedabad, 1944, p. 45.

The instinctive forces of Nature that play a vital role in the life of man, necessitate a control and transformation by means of self-discipline and self-love that ultimately serve as shields for normal awakening of good sense and sensibilities. The seeds of humanism are thus allowed to grow and thrive uninterrupted under the umbrella of mutual love and co-operation. The history of man is, therefore, a striving eternal for the advancement of harmonisation of humanity through mutual love and co-operation. In the words of Gandhi,

> Mutual love enables Nature to persist. Man does not live by destruction. Self-love compels regard for others. Nations cohere because there is mutual regard among individuals composing them. Some day we must extend the national law to the universe, even as we have extended the family law to form nations – a larger family.

> – M.K. Gandhi: *Young India*, March 2, 1922, p. 130.

The history of man is one of progress of mankind – an awakening of all – *Sarvodaya*, – from crudities of life. Violence is being gradually replaced by non-violence, untruth by truth. Man marks his own victory of his own self through evolution and understanding of the spirit of *Sarvodaya*. The spirit within is the spirit that fosters this spirit of humanism. Gandhi characteristically portrays this history of humanism from the standpoint of *Sarvodaya*:

> Our remote ancestors were cannibals. Then came a time when they were fed up with cannibalism and they began to live on chase. Next came a stage when man was ashamed of leading the life of a wandering hunter. He therefore took to agriculture and depended principally on mother earth for his food. Thus from being a nomad he settled down to civilised stable life, founded villages and towns, and from member of a family he became member of a community and a nation. All these are signs of progressive *ahimsa* and diminishing *himsa*. Had it been otherwise, the human species

> should have been extinct by now, even as many of the lower species have disappeared.
>
> Prophets and *avatars* have also taught the lesson of *ahimsa* more or less. Not one of them has professed to teach *himsa*. And how should it be otherwise? *Himsa* does not need to be taught. Man as animal is violent, but as spirit is non-violent. The moment he awakes to the spirit within, he cannot remain violent. Either he progresses towards *ahimsa* or rushes to his doom. That is why the prophets and *avatars* have taught the lesson of truth, harmony, brotherhood, justice, etc. – all attributes of *ahimsa*.
>
> And yet violence seems to persist. . . . If we believe that mankind has steadily progressed towards *ahimsa*, it follows that it has to progress towards it still further. Nothing in this world is static, everything is kinetic. If there is no progression, then there is inevitable retrogression. No one can remain without the eternal cycle, unless it be God Himself.
>
> – M.K. Gandhi : *Harijan*, August 11, 1940, p. 245.

The advancement of humanism through *Sarvodaya* has also its basis on self-realisation, for self-realisation is the keypoint of being blessed with the nearness to God. As an humble servant of mankind, Gandhi says about himself:

> If I found myself entirely absorbed in the service of the community, the reason behind it was my desire for self-realisation. I had made the religion of service my own, as I felt that God could be realised only through service. And service for me was the service for India, because it came to me without my seeking, because I had an aptitude for it. I had gone to South Africa for travel, for finding an escape from Kathiawad intrigues and for gaining my own livelihood. But as I have said, I found myself in search of God and striving for self-realisation.
>
> – M.K. Gandhi: *An Autobiography*, Navajivan Publishing House, Ahmedabad, 1948, p. 197.

What is the most poignant avenue of the search for God ? How can a person be in unison with the will of God ? According to Gandhi, the avenue of looking within is to visualise God who is omnipresent. It is the striving for self-purification through self-realisation by which a person looks within and looks with satisfaction for the awakening of the soul-force in him directs him towards the welfare of all for the welfare of himself.

How is individual welfare turned into the welfare of the community? How can physical labour be heightened to humanistic welfare? How can the spirit of *Sarvodaya* be enkindled by means of 'bread labour' as Gandhi expresses? Gandhi justifies undergoing physical labour from the standpoint of *Sarvodaya* as the 'highest form of sacrifice' for humanism:

> Brahma created his people with the duty of sacrifice laid upon them and said, 'By this do you flourish. Let it be the fulfiller of all our desires'. . . He who eats without performing this sacrifice eats stolen bread", – thus says the *Gita*, 'Earn thy bread by the sweet of thy brow', says the *Bible*. Sacrifices may be of many kinds. One of them may well be Bread labour. If all laboured for their bread and no more, then there would be enough food and enough leisure for all. Then there would be no cry of over-population, no disease and no such misery as we see around. Such labour will be the highest form of sacrifice. Men will no doubt do many other things either through their bodies or through their minds, but all this will be labour of love for the common good.
>
> – M.K. Gandhi: *Harijan*, June 29, 1935, p. 156.

Physical labour turned into labour of love 'for the common good' might be an unattainable ideal, but who denies that for the best efflorescence of humanism we cannot but follow that ideal? As Gandhi adds,

> This may be an unattainable ideal. But we need not, therefore, cease to strive for it. Even if without fulfilling the whole law of sacrifice, that, the law of our being, we performed physical labour enough for our daily bread, we should go a long way towards the

ideal.

> If we did so, our wants would be minimised, our food would be simple. We should then eat to live, not live to eat. Let anyone who doubts about the accuracy of this proposition try to sweat for his bread, he will derive the greatest relish from the productions of his labour, improve his health and discover that many things he took were superfluities.
>
> —*Ibid.*

Elsewhere, Gandhi makes a prophetic appeal to the emergence of humanism by means of encouraging labours as the essence of simplicity and love:

> Bread labour is a variable blessing to one who would observe Non-violence, worship Truth and make the observants of *brahmacharya* a natural act.
>
> . . . Everyone must be his own scavenger. Evacuation is as necessary as eating; and the best thing would be for everyone to dispose of his own waste. If this is impossible, each family should see to its own scavenging. I have felt for years, that there must be something radically wrong, where scavenging has been made the concern of a separate class in society. We have no historical record of the man, who first assigned the lowest status to this essential sanitary service. Whoever he was, he by no means did us a good. We should from our very childhood, have the idea impressed upon our minds that we are all scavengers, and the easiest way of doing so is, for everyone who has realised this, to commence Bread labour as a scavenger. Scavenging, thus intelligently taken up, will help one to a true appreciation of the equality of man.
>
> – M.K. Gandhi: *From Yeravda Mandir*, Navajivan Press, Ahmedabad 1935, p. 50

Looking upon every work as worship of the All Beautiful is no doubt a great inner awakening for which Gandhi always advocates. He also harps on an abiding sense of duty for everyone of us, which eliminates all petty thoughts of differences and misconceptions. Also, it eliminates class distinction and at the same time allows individuality to thrive in freedom for the real emergence of humanism, Professor V.K.R.V. Rao highlights this aspect of *Sarvodaya* very characteristically:

> Sarvodaya, the welfare of all, is a classless society based on the destruction of the classes but not on the destruction of the individuals who constitute the classes, a system of production that does not fail to make use of science and technology for creating an economy of abundance but does not in the process either kill individual initiative or freedom for development or create a psychology of ceaseless striving for more and more material goods, a system of distribution that will ensure a reasonable minimum income for all, and while not aiming at a universal equality of an arithmetical kind, will nevertheless ensure that all private property or talent beyond the minimum will be used as a trust for the public good and not for individual aggrandisement, a social order where all will work but there is no inequality, either in status or in opportunity for any individual, and a political system where change is the result of persuasion, differences are resolved by discussion, and conflict by love and recognition of mutuality of interest and a life spent in dedication to God and cultivation of the spirit.
>
> – V.K.R.V. Rao: *The Gandhian Alternative to Western Socialism*, Bharatiya Vidya Bhavan, Bombay, p. 47.

For a *Sarvodaya* society of humanistic endeavour, the basic point of interest is disinterestedness in amassing wealth, power and position. This will also lead to gradual extinction of attraction even for individuality, for an individual, in the meanwhile, will be prized with the contentment of austerity. Gandhi makes a very significant remark on the unison of the individual and the community from the standpoint of morality:

> There is not a single virtue which aims at, or is content with, the welfare of the individual alone. Conversely, there is not a single moral offence which does not, directly or indirectly, affect many others besides the actual offender. Hence, whether an individual is

> good or bad is not merely His own concern, but really the concern of the whole community, nay of the whole world.
>
> – M.K. Gandhi: *Ethical Religion*, S. Ganesan Triplicane, Madras, 1928, p. 55.

To be enkindled with the spirit of dedication towards humanity is always the focal point of *Sarvodaya.* To create a harmony of conflicting forces in human behavioural designs demands an initiation into the inherent spirit of *sarvodaya.* For this the minimum requirement for a genuine human society is to enjoy equal rights, opportunities and efflorescence of freedom. While reaching self-sufficiency, care should also be taken to allow natural development of human qualities to foster international co-operation. A consolidated approach to humanism based on the principle of *Sarvodaya* as Gandhi conceives is the only one for the real oneness of mankind. As Prem Kirpal observes,

> Gandhi measured progress in terms of human happiness. He wanted a society in which every man would have equal status, opportunity and freedom to develop. He wanted a simple society in which economic progress and social justice would go together. He was not opposed to material prosperity nor did he reject the use of machines in all circumstances. He did not want man to become a slave of the machine and lose his identity altogether; he wanted machines to be for men, not men for machines. He disliked the waste and selfishness that are often generated by growing affluence and accumulation of wealth. If he sought for economic and social development, it was to enrich the quality of life in terms of human happiness and the quest for the moral and spiritual transcendence of man.
>
> Self-reliance dictated his essential approach to development, yet self-sufficiency was not to be aimed at to the exclusion of international cooperation. The relevance of this approach is evident today. For, ideally, the developed and the developing countries should be partners and comrades in common tasks contributing to the increasing solidarity of mankind. In order to make development meaningful for the whole of humanity we must strive to impart a moral character to the acts of giving and receiving in the material

world; the success of this effort will lead us to the road towards a new humanism.

According to Gandhi, we must do everything possible to develop a feeling for the oneness of mankind through reverence for the spirit of man and the practice of the great virtue the compassion. This will indeed be the surest foundation of the new humanism, deriving its strength from all great religions and traditions, gaining from the scientific spirit of our times, and becoming ultimately something like a new religion of the future. With truth and non-violence as his guiding stars, man was Gandhi's recurring theme.

– Prem Kirpal: "Truth and Non-violence in Gandhi's Humanism": *Truth and Non-violence* Gandhi Peace Foundation, New Delhi on behalf of Indian National Commission for Co-operation with UNESCO, New Delhi 1970, pp. 29-31.

To establish 'a Kingdom of God on earth', a kingdom of kingdom through observance of the spirit of *Sarvodaya* as Gandhi wants, is to make room for broadness of humanistic outlook. It is also to make room for the way of thought pure and serene to orient life from ethical and aesthetic points of view. The whole world is embraced in the chords of love and beauty. It disçards all littleness and allows the warmth of life to be enjoyed and shared in vastness of outlook. As professor Mahadevan observes,

Sarvodaya is both a way of thought and a way of life. . . . As a way of thought *Sarvodaya* exhorts man not to think of himself in isolation from the rest of creation but to feel convinced of his oneness with all. No individual can really rise on the depression of others. What every member of society should aim at is common weal, the welfare of the whole, for all are aspects of one Reality, expressions of one Spirit. As a way of life, *Sarvodaya* stands for co-sharing and co-operation instead of mad race for accumulation through competition and aggression; for peaceful and non-violent progress instead of chaotic existence under the constant threat of dread and destruction. *Sarvodaya* is the gospel of wholeness; and in this space age, there is no real alternative to it.

> – Prof. T.M.P. Mahadevan: Introduction: *N.K. Reddy: Sarvodaya Ideology and Acharya,* The A.P. Sarvodaya Mandal, Hyderabad 1963.

The inherent spirit of *Sarvodaya* as a way of life has, as Gandhi thinks, its basis on an integrated approach to life from manifold aspects of human development – moral, material and spiritual. It is, therefore, unjust to say that a man's development should be merely geared to moral or spiritual development, nor can human progress be measured without material development. It is a synchronised endeavour to arrive at a point of total development of personality. *Sarvodaya* has its embracing role for the march of humanism. In fact,

> . . . When Gandhi championed the cause of *Sarvodaya*, he not merely had before him the objective of welfare of all, but also all round welfare of all the individuals in the society that embraces ethical and spiritual development, as much as material development.

> – Benudhar Pradhan: "The Socialist Thought of Mahatma Gandhi", *Gandhi*, GDK Publications, Delhi. Vol. 1, Ch. 5, p. 312.

Sarvodaya that 'preaches the merging of oneself in the good of all', defies or rather heightens utilitarianism in the sense that it has, in its core, the seeds of true humanism. It preaches the principles and aesthetics of self-sacrifice not from the dogmatic point of view but from the point of view of crystallisation of utilitarian perspectives. Utilitarianism is thus geared to divergent avenues of the welfare of mankind in its totality of perfect vision of humanism:

> The logic of utilitarianism never conceives the possibility of self-sacrifice; its approach to the problem of the greatest good is always in terms of the party whose interest is in question. It gives rise to the problem of minority and majority. On the other hand, self-sacrifice is the very foundation of *Sarvodaya* which preaches

the merging of oneself in the good of all.

– B.S. Sarma: "The Philosophical Basis of Sarvodaya", *Gandhi Marg*, Journal of Gandhi Peace Foundation, New Delhi, Vol. IV, No. 3, July 1960, p. 258.

The spirit of self-sacrifice which is the most essential and inherent spirit of *Sarvodaya* leaves aside materialism and utilitarianism not because there is an essential and specific point of difference in ideology but primarily because humanism has its transcendence from materialism to spiritualism. The god in man – the All Beautiful – awaits emergence and beyonding from both utilitarianism and materialism. Perhaps the humanistic vision of Gandhi is a serene transcendence from the Marxian interpretation of humanism. As J.P. Narayan characteristically observes,

I feel convinced that man must go beyond the material to find the incentive to goodness. As a corollary, I feel further that the task of social reconstruction, cannot succeed under the inspiration of a materialistic philosophy.

– J.P. Narayan: *Socialism to Sarvodaya*, Socialist Book Centre, Madras, 1956, pp. 30-31.

The utilitarian approach to humanism has been oriented to *Sarvodaya* by Gandhi to accelerate it towards purity of thought and action by means of a transcendence from materialism to spiritualism. Mankind cannot but be aware of self-sacrifice which means that everyone must be willing to die so that others might enjoy the warmth of living. The greatest good of everyone as *Sarvodaya* philosophy teaches us paves the avenues of excellence for the inherent man – the man beyond man purified in the broadness of vision. As Gandhi remarks,

A votary of *ahimsa* cannot subscribe to the utilitarian formula (of the greatest good of the greatest member). He will strive for the greatest good of all and die in the attempt to realise the ideal. He will therefore be willing to die, so that the others may live. He will serve himself with the rest, by himself dying. The greatest good of

> all inevitably included the good of the greatest number, and therefore, he and the utilitarian will converge in many points in their career but there does come a time when they must part company, and even work in opposite directions. The utilitarian to be logical will never sacrifice himself. The absolutist will even sacrifice himself.
>
> – M.K. Gandhi: *Young India*, December 8, 1926, p. 432.

As *Sarvodaya* is based on the humanistic principle of *Sarva mangala bhavana* (the thought of the welfare of all), it always caters to the principle of self-purity through thought and action for the goodness of mankind. Gandhi even goes so far so to deny the very approach to the self for survival because he thinks that if a man allows himself to be rest assured with the will of the great Creator as birds, beasts and many other living objects of Nature do for their existence, he can entirely devote himself to the cause of humanism. This is a great principle of self-sacrifice that widens newer avenues of human excellence. As Gandhi observes,

> A seeker after Truth, a follower of the law of Love, cannot hold anything against tomorrow. God never stores for the morrow, He never creates more than what is strictly needed for the moment. If, therefore, we repose faith in His providence, we should rest assured that He will give us everyday, our daily bread, meaning everything that we require. Perfect fulfilment of the ideal of Non-possession requires that man should, like the birds, have no roof over his head, no clothing and no stock of food for the morrow. He will indeed need his daily bread, but it will be God's business, and not his, to provide for it.
>
> – M.K. Gandhi: *From Yeravda Mandir*, Navajivan Press, Ahmedabad, 1935, p. 34.

Elsewhere, Gandhi substantiates the principle of non-possession as the inherent spirit of *Sarvodaya*.

> Every human being has a right to live and therefore, to find the wherewithal to feed himself and where necessary, to clothe and

> house himself. But for this very simple performance we need no assistance from economics or their laws.
>
> 'Take no thought of the morrow' is an injunction which finds an echo in almost all the religious scriptures of the world. In well-ordered society the security of one's livelihood should be and is found to be the easiest thing in the world. Indeed, the rest of orderliness in a country is not the number of millionaires it owns, but the absence of starvation among its masses. The only statement that has to be examined is whether it can be laid down as a law of universal application that material advancement means moral progress.
>
> – M.K. Gandhi: *Speeches and Writings of Mahatma Gandhi*, G.A. Natesan & Co., Madras, p. 350.

As for specific instance, Gandhi makes a global overview of 'Moral fall' in the event of 'material affluence' that betrays *Sarvodaya* and, for that end in view, efflorescence of humanism:

> Rome suffered a moral fall when it attained high material affluence. So did Egypt and so perhaps most countries of which we have any historical record. The descendants and kinsmen of the royal and divine Krishna too fell when they were rolling in riches. We do not deny to the Rockefellers and the Carnegies possession of an ordinary measure of morality but we gladly judge them indulgently. I mean that we do not even expect them to satisfy the highest standard of morality. With them material gain has not necessarily meant moral gain. In South Africa, where I had the privilege of associating with thousands of our countrymen on most intimate terms, I observed almost invariably that the greater the possession of riches, the greater was their moral turpitude. Our rich men, to say the least, did not advance the moral struggle of passive resistance as did the poor. The rich men's sense of self-respect was not so much injured as that of the poorest. If I were not afraid of treading on dangerous ground, I would even come nearer home and show how that possession of riches has been a hindrance to real growth. I venture to think that the scriptures of the world are far safer and sounder treatises on laws of economics than many of the

modern textbooks.

—*Ibid.*

The economic disparities between the rich and the poor that actually stand in the way of *Sarvodaya* has pained Gandhi so much as to forewarn an impending global revolution for the cause of goodness for mankind. The social imbalances as existent to overpower the spirit of *Sarvodaya* cannot but act as a boomerang for the common good of humanity. While introducing his scheme of constructive programme for the cause of the common goodness of mankind, Gandhi makes a prophetic warning:

> Working for economic equality means abolishing the eternal conflict between capital and labour. It means the levelling down of the few rich in whose hands is concentrated the bulk of the nation's wealth on the one hand, and a levelling-up of the semi-starved naked millions on the other. A non-violent system of government is clearly an impossibility so long as the wide gulf between the rich and the hungry millions persists. The contrast between the palaces of New Delhi and the miserable hovels of the poor labouring class cannot last one day in a free India in which the poor will enjoy the same power as the richest in the land. A violent and bloody revolution is a certainty one day unless there is a voluntary abdication of riches and the power that riches give and sharing them for the common good.
>
> — M.K. Gandhi: *Constructive Programme: Its Meaning and Place*, Navajivan Press, Ahmedabad, 1944, p. 18.

Non-possession, as Gandhi considers to be an invaluable component of *Sarvodaya*, also advances the spirit of humanism. To be really justified to humanity is, according to him, to remain above the petty self with all its materialistic and schizophrenic approach to life; with the conquest of desire, man, as Gandhi emphasises, purifies his little self to be in unison with the higher self that merges in the good of one and all:

> It has been truly said, that desire for enjoyment creates bodies for

> the soul, when this desire vanishes, there remains no further need for the body, and man is free from the vicious cycle of births and deaths. The soul is omnipresent; why should she care to be contained within the cage-like body, or do evil and even kill for the sake of that cage? We thus arrive at the ideal of total renunciation, and learn to use the body for the purposes of service so long as it exists, so much so that service, and not bread, becomes with us the staff of life. We eat and drink, sleep and wake, for service alone. Such an attitude of mind brings us happiness, and the beatific vision in the fulness of time.
>
> – M.K. Gandhi: *From Yeravda Mandir*, Navajivan Press, Ahmedabad 1935, p. 37.

How can service towards mankind be enriched? How can mankind be worthy of the purified inner vision that awaits efflorescence? A Sarvodayite knows well that he should be prepared for any sacrifice whatsoever for the cause of humanism. He prepares himself, bit by bit, to be perfect in, and worthy of any action he undertakes for the all-round welfare of humanity. His shield is strict morality, his weapon, self-resistance. He welcomes any suggestion that promotes humanism and decries any abuse of power and possession that speedily eat up all endeavour for the inner growth of mankind. He adorns himself with the truth of the great Upanisadic dictum *tena tyektena bhunjitha*, — glorify thyself by self-sacrifice — and strengthen himself with the great inner force of morality. As an ardent champion of humanism, Gandhi formulates his vision of *Sarvodaya* on moral laws and principles in order to discharge duties and responsibilities for the good of all. As he characteristically observes,

> Our desires and motives may be divided into two classes — selfish and unselfish. All selfish desires are immoral, while the desire to improve ourselves for the sake of doing good to others is truly moral. The highest moral law is that we should unremittingly work for the good of mankind.
>
> – M.K. Gandhi : *Ethical Religion*, S. Ganesan, Triplicane, Madras, 1930, p. 36.

The religion of humanism is the religion of *Sarvodaya*, the religion of true morality inseparably interwined. One who is initiated with the true spirit of religion is also enkindled with the true spirit of *Sarvodaya* for *Sarvodaya* is the outcome of the union of morality and religion which are inseparable. In the words of Gandhi,

> As soon as we lose the moral basis, we cease to be religious. There is no such thing as religion overriding morality. Man for instance, cannot be untruthful, cruel and incontinent and claim to have God on his side.
>
> – M.K. Gandhi : *Young India*, November 24, 1921, p. 385.

Sarvodaya, the image of the inner man as man should be for all time to come, is the only hope of regeneration of humanism. When will we rise up as one man to be justified to this incomparable principle of Gandhian Humanism?

6

NON-VIOLENCE AND GANDHIAN HUMANISM

THE GREATEST worth of man is that he has the incomparable and extraordinary power to exceed himself. He has a puny body, no doubt, but he has a mighty heart within that puny body — the heart that excels and exceeds, lightens and is lighted. He has a vision — a vision of beyonding — and when he is absorbed in that vision, he is christened with the warmth of the inner spirit.

How is the warmth of the inner spirit felt ? What is the strategic force that acts and reacts within man ? How is a man confronted with the conflicting forces that bring about a crusade of crossfire within him?

A humanist *par excellence,* Gandhi finds the source-point of humanism in non-violence, which, according to him, bears a long tradition. It is nothing new because the spirit of non-violence is dormant in every human being. This necessitates a spurt to be ignited, a method to be practised in perfect harmony and poignance. Moreover, as non-violence is rooted to our ancient culture and tradition, it merely awaits a move anew for better awakening of humanistic awareness. Gandhi elucidates the truth from a new angle of vision and foretells on the salvation of a battered world through non-violence :

> The religion of non-violence is not meant merely for the *rishis* and saints. It is meant for the common people as well. Non-violence is the law of our species as violence is the law of the brute. The spirit lies dormant in the brute and he knows no law but that of physical might. The dignity of man requires obedience to a higher law — to the strength of the spirit.
>
> I have therefore ventured to place before India the ancient law of self-sacrifice. For, *satyagraha* and its off shoots, non-cooperation and civil resistance, are nothing but new names

> for the law of suffering. The *rishis*, who discovered the law of non-violence in the midst of violence, were greater geniuses that Newton. They were themselves greater warriors than Wellington. Having themselves known the use of arms, they realised their uselessness and taught a weary world that its salvation lay not through violence but through non-violence.
>
> — M. K. Gandhi : *Young India*, August 11, 1920, p. 712.

A 'soul force' as Tolstoy terms non-violence, it is a sort of resistance that has its roots within. It calls forth justice not in law enforced, but in law realised from the care of the heart. Gandhi emphasises on imposition of the principles of non-violence by shutting the inner will of the mind — the will of doing good to mankind. As he remarks.

> Passive resistance is a method of securing rights by personal suffering; it is the reverse of resistance by arms. When I refuse to do a thing that is repugnant to my conscience, I use soul-force. For instance, the Government of the day has passed a law which is applicable to me. I do not like it. If by using violence I force the Government to repeat the law, I am employing what may be termed body-force. If I do not obey the law and accept the penalty for its breach, I use soul-force. It involves sacrifice of self.
>
> Everybody admits that sacrifice of self is infinitely superior to sacrifice of other. Moreover, if this kind of force is used in a cause that is unjust, only the person using it suffers. He does not make others suffer for his mistakes. Men have before now done many things which were subsequently found to have been wrong. No man can claim that he is absolutely in the right or that a particular thing is wrong because he thinks so, but it is wrong for him so long as that is his deliberate judgment. It is therefore meet that he should not do that which he knows to be wrong, and suffer the consequence whatever it may be. This is the key to the use of soul-force.
>
> — M. K. Gandhi : *Hind Swaraj or Indian Home Rule*, Navajivan Publishing House, Ahmedabad, 1944, p. 45.

Action based an contemplation of the consequence is the ethical background of Gandhian non-violence. Gandhi, therefore, uses the soul-force to eliminate body-force or any other force that only welcomes chaos and stands in the way of inner harmony. Indeed, non-violence, as Gandhi conceives, is a continual revolution that goes within for the cause of humanism. It does not allow untoward force to creep in the mind and destroy the conscience of the welfare of mankind. It does not allow the mind to veer like the wings of a compass under the strong influence of the little 'I' that dwarfs the greater 'I' within every human being. It does not allow to dole out good sense and sensibility to fulfil initial material gains. When Gandhi introduces the movement of non-cooperation he basically gives a new meaning to the word or concept of 'revolution', widening it towards humane perspectives. As he explicitly spells out :

> Hitherto the word 'revolution' has been connected with violence and has as such been condemned by established authority. But the movement of non-cooperation, if it may be considered a revolution, is not an armed revolt; it is an evolutionary revolution, it is a bloodless revolution. The movement is a revolution of thought, of spirit. Non-cooperation is a process of purification, and, as such, it constitutes a revolution in one's ideas. Its suppression, therefore, would amount to cooperation by coercion. Orders to kill the movement will be orders to destroy, or interfere with, the introduction of the spinning wheel, to prohibit the campaign of temperance, and an incitement, therefore, to violence. For attempt to compel people by indirect methods to wear foreign clothes, to patronise drink-shops would certainly exasperate them. But our success will be assured when we stand even the exasperation and incitement. We must not retort. Inaction on our part will kill Government madness. For violence flourishes on response either by submission to the will of the violator, or by counter-violence. My strong advice to every worker is to segregate this evil Government by street non-cooperation, not even to talk or speak about it, but having recognised the evil, to cease to pay homage to it by cooperation.
>
> — M. K. Gandhi : *Young India*, March 30, 1921, p. 91.

For the inner victory of man, non-violence as Gandhi believes, never means inaction even when action serves the greater and nobler purpose of humanity. In fact, he is inspired by the *Gita* that teaches him how to act — a lesson which is 'The essence of truthful living.' G. Ramachandran highlights this point when he reacts to the misinterpretation of an oft-quoted statement of Gandhi :

> I do believe that where there is only a choice between cowardice and violence I would advise violence . . . I would rather have India resort to arms in order to defend her honour than that she should, in a cowardly manner become or remain a helpless witness to her own dishonour.
>
> — *Young India*, August 15, 1920

and observes as follows :

> I listened with profound interest to what professor Hersch* said about Gandhi's oftquoted statement, that 'where there is only a choice between cowardice and violence, I would advise violence, She described it as 'a way of speaking'. Gandhi ends that statement by saying, 'But I believe that non-violence is infinitely superior to violence'. I have tried to study the thought behind this statement for a long time and I have come to the conclusion that for Gandhi the first imperative is action — and then the inescapable second is non-violence. This comes straight out of the *Gita*. In my opinion, there is no non-violence in the *Gita*. But there is in the *Gita* the challenge to action in the face of a situation. It is symbolised in two figures — Krishna and Arjuna. Arjuna drops his weapons and says, 'I do not want to fight, because it means the killing of so many of my kith and kin'. Krishna says, 'Take up your weapons and fight because it is your duty to fight'. Out of the *Gita*, Gandhi got the lesson that action is the essence of truthful living.
>
> — G. Ramachandran: "The Relations of Truth and Non-violence in Gandhi's thinking", *Truth and Non-violence* Ed. by T. K. Mahadevan, Gandhi Peace Foundation on behalf of Indian National Commission for co-operation with UNESCO, New Delhi, 1970, p. 130.

* Jeanne Hersch: Professor of Philosophy, University of Geneva, Switzerland. Former Director, Division of Philosophy, UNESCO.

As a close associate of Gandhi for a long time, G. Ramachandran, who spent 1926 with Gandhi in the Satyagraha Ashram at Sabarmati, adds :

> Gandhi was once talking to some of us in the Sevagram Ashram and, as far as I remember, these were his words : 'You might follow the Ten Commandments of the *Bible*. You might even follow the 101 commandments of Gandhi—put on *khadi*, touch no liquor, serve the untouchable, etc. etc. — but if the challenge of a moral action came to you and you evaded it, then all the other disciplines to which you gave allegiance are wiped out altogether and you have committed moral and spiritual suicide.' The first imperative of Gandhi was to act — here, now, in the living present — against injustice and evil. In doing so, his inevitable corollary was that action to be truly effective must be non-violent. So when he said, 'where there is only a choice between cowardice and violence, I would advise violence', he was expressing his passionate conviction that there must be action, not words, not thought, in the face of a contingency. As Prof. Hersch said, this was his way of clearing non-violence from the odium that it is inaction, cowardice and running away. . . .
>
> The fundamental issue confronting us is; can we have humanism without non-violence ? Gandhi's answer was crystal clear. He had no doubt whatsoever in his mind that we would never achieve true humanism except through non-violence. We have had instances of freedom being achieved through violence. It is not as though freedom has never been achieved through violence. But whether humanism has been achieved anywhere in the world through violence is a question we must face without equivocation.
>
> We have had two world wars and we may well be on the threshold of a third world war. It is idle to imagine that, having stockpiled weapons of incalculable distructive power and with the super powers all the time jostling against each other for the dominance of the world, these weapons would never be used. Can any one tell me why untold wealth and technique and effort are put into the production of these weapons and then they sit down together to find out how best *not to use them* ? If this is not senile idiocy, I do not know what it is. It is in the face of this absurd

situation that Gandhi's challenge comes.

—*Ibid.*, pp. 132-133.

A practical way of escaping annihilation of mankind, non-violence as Gandhi teaches us, shows how to face any eventuality of life. In this connection, Ramachandran makes a very poignant observation :

> People imagine that non-violence is very difficult and costly to the person who gives allegiance to it. But is violence cheap ? Is defence through armaments cheap ? Will not millions perish ? Has it not been calculated that within 24 hours of a nuclear war, 150 millions of people on either side, men, women and children, would die ? Is it a cheap price to pay ? Instead of paying that price of mutually destroying each other, Gandhi said, 'Let us face death without flinching'. Let me conclude by saying that in the economy of God's wisdom, non-violence is more practical, more effective and perhaps the only way of escaping the total annihilation that confronts us today.

—*Ibid.*, p. 133.

Looking upon the world as a mysterious platform for assessment of human sensibilities, Gandhi motivates the whole of mankind towards his principle of non-violence not because he hates destruction, disintegration, violence or hatred but because he badly wants to make every living being aware of the worth of living. That every human being is blessed with the unique and unconquerable spirit of excellence of higher vision of life as ordained by God within is the great force that non-violence initiates in mankind. Gandhi points towards this positive aspect of non-violence as a great humanistic force. When non-violence is directed towards this positive aspect of humanism love takes a major role to embrace and do good even to the wrongdoer. But, then, non-violence might often go beyond mere resistance and take the form of action, if necessary. As he clarifies through his own interpretation of *ahimsa,*

> I accept the interpretation of *ahimsa,* namely, that it is not merely a negative state of harmlessness but it is a positive state of love,

> of doing good even to the evil-doer. But it does not mean helping the evil-doer to continue the wrong or tolerating it by passive acquiescence on the contrary, love, the active state of *ahimsa*, requires. you to reset the wrong-doer by dissociating yourself from him even though it may offend him or injure him physically.
>
> — M. K. Gandhi : *Young India*, August 25, 1920, p. 322.

The inherent humanistic force of non-violence that works in Gandhi's mind is that it is 'the mightiest weapon' of destruction of evil forces only to bring harmony and unity in mankind. As he elucidates more characteristically,

> It (non-violence) is mightier than the mightiest weapon of destruction devised by the ingenuity of man. Destruction is not the law of the humans. Man lives freely by his readiness to die, if need be, at the hands of his brother, never by killing him. Every murder or other injury, no matter for what cause committed or inflicted on another is a crime against humanity.
>
> — R. K. Prabhu & U. R. Rao : *The Mind of Mahatma Gandhi*, Oxford University Press, London, 1945, p. 49.

The violence or destruction has almost become the creed of life. Gandhi introduces *ahimsa* to counteract with violence not merely to resist it but also to practise the positive approach to life. This means that to conquer violence is to take recourse to non-violence through love. Let the force of non-violence teach the lesson to all mankind that life to be worth living needs a genuine sense of mutual cooperation and harmony. And, for this, love acts as a guiding principle. A superhuman mystic spirit that one receives from that of love guides the non-violent worker to negotiate all inconsistencies of humanity. Gandhi's own interpretation of love as a guiding force of non-violence is :

> I have found that life persists in the midst of destruction and therefore there must be a higher law than that of destruction. Only under that law would a well-ordered society be intelligible and life worth living. And if that is the law of life, we have to work it out in daily life. Whenever there are jars, wherever you are confronted with an opponent conquer him with love — in this

> crude manner I have worked it out in my life. That does not mean that all my difficulties are solved. Only I have found that this law of love has answers as the law of destruction has never done.
>
> It is not that I am incapable of anger, for instance, but I succeed on almost all occasions to keep my feelings under control. Whatever may be the result, there is always in me conscious struggle for following the law of non-violence deliberately and ceaselessly. Such a struggle leaves one stronger for it. The more I work at this law, the more I feel the delight in life, the delight in the scheme of the universe. It gives me a peace and a meaning of the mysteries of nature that I have no power to describe.
>
> — M. K. Gandhi : *Young India,* October 1, 1931, p. 286.

The art of dying as non-violence teaches mankind, has a greater power than violence which grows out of fear. Gandhi averts the strategy of violence because it breeds fear and always tries to be emancipated from fear that escalates anyhow. He prefers to be non-violent in approach because to be non-violent is to be free from the inhibition of fear that eats up the inner growth of humanism. A sense of disinterested attitude towards action and consequences therefrom allows the non-violent crusader to serve humanity as best as possible. Gandhi elucidates the point as follows :

> Just as one must learn the art of killing in the training for violence, so one must learn the art of dying in the training for non-violence. Violence does not mean emancipation from fear, but discovering the means of combating the course of fear. . . . The votary of non-violence has to cultivate the capacity of sacrifice of the highest type in order to be free from fear. He recks not if he should lose his land, his wealth, his life. He who has not overcome all fear cannot practise *ahimsa* to perfection.
>
> — M. K. Gandhi : *Harijan,* September 1, 1940, p. 268.

As Gandhi gives little importance to external fear that tempts one to take recourse to violence, he does not think that violence can win over internal fear, — the fear of being accountable to God for one's wrong doing. He, therefore, emphasises on non-violence that brings forth protection of the self for the cause of humanism :

> The votary of *ahimsa* has only one fear, that is of God. He who seeks refuge in God ought to have a glimpse of the *Atman* that transcends the body; and the moment one has a glimpse of the Imperishable *Atman* one sheds the love of the perishable body. Training in non-violence is thus diametrically opposed to training in violence. Violence is needed for the protection of things external, non-violence is needed for the protection of the *Atman*, for the protection of one's honour.
>
> — *Ibid.*

How to be aware of the *Atman* that heralds the glory of mankind ? Gandhi's answer is that everyone must win over all vicissitudes and disbeliefs with regard to non-violence which is not meant for the limited few but for the whole of mankind. While dispelling the doubt that non-violence as a promoter of humanism is meant only for the few, Gandhi categorically states :

> I claim that even now, though the social structure is not based on a conscious acceptance of non-violence, all the world over mankind lives and men retain their possessions on the sufferance of one another. If they had not done so, only the fewest and the most ferocious would have survived. But such is not the case. Families are bound together by ties of love, and so are groups in the so-called civilised society called nations. Only they do not recognise the supremacy of the law of non-violence. It follows, therefore, that they have not investigated its vast possibilities. Hitherto out of sheer inertia, shall I say, we have taken it for granted that complete non-violence is possible only for the few who take the vow of non-possession and the allied abstinences. Whilst it is true that the votaries alone can carry on research work and declare from time to time the new possibilities of the great eternal law governing man, if it is a law, it must hold good for all.
>
> — M. K. Gandhi : *Harijan*, February 22, 1942, p. 48.

Gandhi also explains the failure of non-violence with a well-drawn simile and concludes with extraordinary humility that in introducing and translating non-violence he is merely a seeker of humanism :

> The many failures we see are not of the law but of the followers, many of whom do not even know that they are under that law willy nilly. When a mother dies for her child she unknowingly obeys the law. I have been pleading for the past fifty years for a conscious acceptance of the law and its zealous practice even in the face of failures. Fifth years' work has shown marvellous results and strengthened my faith. I do claim that by constant practice we shall come to a state of things when lawful possession will command universal and voluntary respect. No doubt such possession will not be tainted. It will not be an insolent demonstration of the inequalities that surround us everywhere. Nor need for problem of unjust and unlawful possession appeal the votary of non-violence. He has at his disposal the non-violent weapon of *Satyagraha* and non-cooperation which hitherto has been found to be a complete substitute of violence whenever it has been applied honesty in sufficient measure. I have never claimed to present the complete science of non-violence. It does not lend itself to such treatment. So far as I know, no single physical science does, not even the very exact science of mathematics. I am a seeker.
>
> —*Ibid.*

In his experience on non-violence, Gandhi sticks to truth only to win over violence through sympathy and patience. The force that the promoter of non-violence receives out of these two humane qualities is one of self-suffering. Therefore, it is a gradual process of transformation that a non-violent person applied his inherent qualities of patience and sympathy to eliminate the errors and evils of violence. Gandhi's own findings are :

> In the application of *Satyagraha*, I discovered in the earliest stages that pursuit of truth did not admit of violence being inflicted on one's opponent but he must be weaned from error by patience and sympathy. For, what appears to be Truth to the one may appear to be error to another. And patience means self-suffering. So the doctrine came to mean vindication of Truth, not by application of suffering on the opponent, but on the one's self.
>
> — M. K. Gandhi : *Young India*, November, 1919.

The 'finest quality of the heart' as Gandhi considers, non-violence acts deep into the heart till all imperfections and impurities are not erased out. It is, therefore, an unending process of mankind to enrich humanism. It caters to all the serene qualities of the head and the heart to be synchronised for the great union with the All Beautiful. In fact, it is a continual process of looking within and looking askance at failures and perfection as well. It encounters all experiences in a broadened vision of awareness for the good eternal. Even when Gandhi thinks of non-violence in terms of the oppressor or the ruler blinded by violence he is aware of the great truth of humanism that man is to be rescued from all inconsistencies and pitfalls. In his corrections of the *Congress Responsibility for the Disturbances*, an 86-page booklet published by the then British Government during his fast, he observes on non-violence from this standpoint of humanism :

> Its (non-violence's) spread in all walks of life has been my mission from early youth. This covers a period of very nearly sixty years. It was adopted at my instance as a policy by the Congress in 1920. In its very nature it was not meant to be paraded before the world, but it was accepted as a means indispensable for the attainment of swaraj. Congressmen saw at an early date that its mere adoption on paper had no value. It was of use only in so far as it was put into practice individually and collectively. It was of no more use as a badge that a rifle in the hands of a person who did not know how to use it effectively on due occasion. Therefore, if non-violence has raised the congress prestige and popularity since its adoption, it has done so in exact proportion to its use, even as the power which the rifle gives to its possessor is in exact proportion to its effective use. The comparison cannot be carried very far. Thus while violence is directed towards the injury, including the distruction, of aggressor, and is successful only when it is stronger than that of the opponent, the non-violent action can be taken in respect of an opponent, however powerfully organised for violence. Violence *per se* of the weak has never been known to succeed against the stronger in violence. Success of non-violent action of the very weak is a daily occurrence. I make bold to say that I have applied to the present struggle the principles of non-violence as enunciated here. Nothing could be further from my thought than injury to the person or property of those who are manning and

> regulating the machinery of British imperialism as it operates in India. My non-violence draws a fundamental distinction between the man and his machine. I would destroy a harmful machine without compunction, never the man.
>
> — D.G. Tendulkar : *Mahatma*, Publications Division, Ministry of Information and Broadcasting, Government of India. Vol. VI, pp. 224-225.

The great humanistic principle that Gandhi teaches through non-violence, is to love everyone and to love also those who hate us. This is undoubtedly a very difficult task to perform but one's earnest endeavour to stick to non-violence gradually leads one to eliminate the hatred of the hater through love. It is the only strategy to uphold Truth which stands for God. When Gandhi speaks of *Satyagraha*, he has a firm conviction that it will triumph over all hindrances. As he is a great humanist, he expresses his faith in *Satyagraha* which he sincerely believes as a spirit within, lying dormant in humanity:

> Non-cooperation and civil disobedience are but different branches of the same tree called *Satyagraha*. — It is my *Kalpadruma* — my Jam-i-Jam — the universal provider. Satyagraha is search for Truth; and God is Truth. Ahimsa or non-violence is the light that reveals that Truth to me. *Swaraj* for me is part of that Truth. This Satyagraha did not fail me in South Africa, Kheda or Champaran and in host of other cases I could mention. It excludes all violence or hate. Therefore, I cannot and will not hate Englishmen. Nor will I bear their yoke. I must fight unto death the unholy attempt to impose British methods and British institutions on India. But I combat the attempt with non-violence. I believe in the capacity of India to offer non-violent battle to the English rulers. The experiment has not failed. It has succeeded, but not to the extent we had hoped and desired. I do not despair. On the contrary, I believe that India will come to her own in the near future, and that only through satyagraha. The proposed suspension is part of the experiment. Non-cooperation need never be resumed if the programme sketched by me can be fulfilled. Non-violent non-cooperation in some form or other, whether through the congress or without it, will be resumed if the programme fails. I have repeatedly stated that *Satyagraha* never fails and that one

> perfect *Satyagrahi* is enough to vindicate Truth. Let us all strive to be perfect *Satyagrahis*. The striving does not require any quality unattainable by the lowliest among us. For *Satyagraha* is an attribute of the spirit within. It is latent in everyone of us. Like *Swaraj* it is our birthright. Let us know it.
>
> — M. K. Gandhi : *Young India*, December 26, 1924.

Looking upon non-violence as the most positive aspect of humanism, Gandhi considers it to be an endless preparation within for perfection. It is an awareness of the eternal values of mankind. Born to suffer in order to purify himself, every man has a responsibility, as Gandhi firmly believes, towards himself and towards mankind as a whole. For this, the person who believes in non-violence banks heavily on modesty for justice denied to him. He is well aware of the fact that love that plays a very significant role in his strategy of non-violence wins in the long run.

Gandhi explains the above-mentioned inherent role of love in non-violent non-co-operation in terms of humanity. Thus sharing others' opinions and making a conjoint endeavour to arrive at Truth through non-violence allows a wider avenue of humanistic advancement. As Gandhi warns,

> The golden rule of conduct . . . is mutual toleration, seeing that we will never all think alike and we shall see *Truth* in fragment and from different angles of vision. Conscience is not the same thing for all. Whilst, therefore, it is a good guide for individual conduct, imposition of that conduct upon all will be an insufferable interference with everybody's freedom of conscience.
>
> — *Ibid.*, September 23, 1926.

In his humanistic approach to non-violence, Gandhi always derides autocracy. He thinks that freedom of individual opinion is actually making a good ground for implementing non-violence. The individual dislikes imposition of any principle however sound it may appear and Gandhi is well aware of this psychological principle of human behaviour. He, therefore, humbly submits about himself as an ardent humanist :

> I have never been able to subscribe to the charge of obstinacy or autocracy. On the contrary, I pride myself on my yielding nature in non-vital matters. I detest autocracy. Valuing my freedom and independence, I equally cherish them for others. I have no desire to carry a single soul with me if I cannot appeal to his or her reason. My unconventionality I carry to the point of rejecting the divinity of the oldest shastras if they cannot convince my reason. But I have found by experience that, if I wish to live in society and still retain my independence, I must limit to the points of utter independences to matters of first rate importance. In all others which do not involve a departure from one's personal religion or moral code, one must yield to the majority.
>
> — M. K. Gandhi : *Young India*, July 14, 1920.

While explaining the pre-requisite for Civil Disobedience Gandhi also expounds the same principle of tolerance as a mark for non-violent humanism. Here, again, he elucidates his point of tolerance with a simile :

> We must tolerate many laws of the State, even when they are inconvenient. A son may not approve of some orders of the father and yet he obeys them. It is only when they are unworthy of tolerance and immoral that he disobeys them. The father will at once understand such respectful disobedience. In the same way it is only when a people have proved their active loyalty by obeying the many laws of the state that they acquire the right of Civil Disobedience.
>
> —*Ibid.*, January 8, 1925.

As a practical humanist, Gandhi banks upon non-violence because it best teaches us how to remain pure in thought and action through non-cooperation. Violence, on the other hand, manifests our utter stupidity and inaction, ignorance and rage. A restrained approach to oddities in life brings forth positive approach too humanism and such an approach cannot but embrace constraints through non-violence. And so whatever provocation appears to be uncontrollable is judiciously bowed down by means of non-cooperation. As Gandhi characteristically remarks,

> Non-violence is the most vital and integral part of non-cooperation. We may fail in everything else and still continue our battle if we remain non-violent. But we capitulate miserably if we fail in adhering to non-violence. Let it be remembered that violence is the keystone of the Government edifice. Since violence is its sheet-anchor and its final refuge, it has rendered itself almost immune from violence on our side by having prepared itself to frustrate all violent effort by the people. We therefore co-operate with the Government in the most active manner when we resort to violence. Any violence on our part must be taken of our stupidity, ignorance and impotent rage. To exercise restraint under the gravest provocation is the truest mark of soldiership. The verest tyro in the art of war knows that he must avoid the ambushes of his adversary. And every provocation is a dangerous ambush into which we must resolutely refuse to walk.
>
> — M. K. Gandhi : *Young India*, July 28, 1921.

A forerunner of humanism as Gandhi is, he categorically asserts that with self-reliance and self-discipline as components of non-violence, a *satyagrahi* creates an incomparable source of strength and ability within himself to encounter any eventuality. He requires more than mere discipline at times because at times he takes the role of a leader from that of a lone soldier of non-violence. A greater depth of vision for humanism within him demands more than being disciplined. He is not only the torch bearer of humanism but also the saviour, the emancipator and the angel of humanistic vision. Gandhi's own elucidation is :

> Discipline has a place in non-violent strategy, but much more is required. In a *Satyagraha* army everybody is a soldier and as a servant. But at a pinch every *Satyagrahi* soldier has also to be his own general and leader. Mere discipline cannot make for leadership. The latter calls for faith and vision.
>
> — M. K. Gandhi : *Harijan*, July 28, 1940.

Moreover,

> Where self-reliance is the order of the day, where no one has to

> look expectantly at another, where there are no leaders and no followers, or where all are leaders and all are followers, the death of a fighter, however eminent, makes not for slackness but on the other hand intensifies the struggle.
>
> — M. K. Gandhi : *Satyagraha in South Africa,* Navajivan Publishing House, Ahmedabad, 1950, p. 288.

An echo of Rabindranath Tagore's great message of humanism *amra savai raja* (We are all kings) is distinctly heard in the extinction of personality as revealed above. Complete self-restraint by means of an earnest approach to non-violence is the best answer to any kind of repression or coersion received from any where and this has become a historical fact in case of Gandhian march for emancipation of humanism. As a humanist, he observes :

> Every movement that survives repression, mild or severe, invariably commands respect which is another name for success. This repression, if we are true, may be treated as a sure sign of the approaching victory. But, if we are true, we shall neither be cowed down nor angrily retaliate and be violent. *Violence is suicide.* Let us recognise that power dies hard, and that it is but natural for the government to make a final effort for life even though it be through repression. Complete self-restraint . . . is the speediest way to success.
>
> — M. K. Gandhi : *Young India,* March 9, 1921.

In analysing the role of a *satyagrahi,* Gandhi also gives a great deal of emphasis on self-suffering and self-sacrifice because he thinks that but for these, a *satyagrahi* ceases to be a *satyagrahi*. Moreover, none can expect that a whole generation cannot be christened in non-violent non-co-operation outright. A few devoted soldiers of humanism forearmed with the weapons of non-violence stir up the movement for emancipation of humanity. Hence, discipline in non-violence. As he observes,

> He who has not the capacity of suffering cannot non-co-operate. He who has not learnt to sacrifice his property and even his family when necessary can never cooperate. It is possible that a

> prince enraged by non-cooperation will inflict all manner of punishment. There lies the test of love, patience, and strength. He who is not ready to undegro the fiery ordeal cannot non-cooperate. A whole people cannot be considered fit or ready for non-cooperation when only an individual or two have mastered these three lessons. A large number of the people must be thus prepared before they can non-cooperate. The result of hasty non-cooperation can only lead to harm. Some patriotic young men who do not understand the limitations noted by me grow impatient. Previous preparation is needed for non-cooperation as it is for all important things. A man cannot become a non-cooperator by merely wishing to be one. Discipline is obligatory.
>
> — M. K. Gandhi, *Young India,* January 8, 1925.

In spite of the fact that all men cannot be oriented or branded as disciplined followers of non-violence abruptly, it is also equally true that a sustained continual and co-ordinated approach to mass orientation for successful launching of non-violence brings forth worthy dividents. Gandhi, therefore, keeps the course of practising non-violence wide open for gradual acceptance and implementation through honest endeavour. As he declares,

> Let no one understand that a non-violent army is open only to those who strictly enforce in their lives all the implications of non-violence. It is open to all those who accept the implications and make an ever-increasing endeavour to observe them. There never will be an army of perfectly non-violent people. It will be formed of those who will honestly endeavour to observe non-violence.
>
> — M. K. Gandhi : *Harijan*, July 21, 1940.

A truth-force as non-violence is, it cannot under any circumstances be subdued for eternity; a force inherent as it is, it will in the long run prize mankind with the victory of humanism. As Gandhi prophetically voices,

> There can be no *Satyagraha* in an unjust cause. *Satyagraha* in a

> just cause is vain, if the men espousing it are determined and capable of fighting and suffering to the end; and the slightest use of violence often defeats a just cause. *Satyagraha* excludes the use of violence in any shape or form, whether in thought, speech, or deed. Given a just cause, capacity for endless suffering and avoidance of violence, victory is a certainty.
>
> — M. K. Gandhi : *Young India*, April 27, 1921.

Perhaps, never is Gandhi so much misunderstood as a humanist as he launches his principle of *satyagraha* in connection with Jalianwala Bagh massacre. The deeply wounded sentinel of humanity is even now misinterpreted due to appalling poverty of informatios and sane reasonings. Here is Gandhi's own verdict :

> The pledge of non-violence does not require us to co-operate in our humiliation. It , therefore, does not require us to crawl on our bellies or to draw lines with our noses or walk to salute the Union Jack or to do anything degrading at the dictation of officials. On the contrary, our creed requires us to refuse to do any of these things even though we should be shot. It was, therefore, for instance, no part of the duty of the Jalianwala Bagh people to run away or even to turn their backs when they were fired upon. If the message of non-violence had reached them, they would have been expected when fire was opened on them to march towards it with bare breasts and die rejoicing in the belief that it meant the freedom of their country. Non-violence laughs at the might of the tyrant and stultifies him by non-retaliation and non-retiral. We played into General Dyer's hands because we acted as he had expected. He wanted us to run away from his fire, he wanted us to crawl on our bellies and to draw lines with our noses. That was a part of the game of 'frightfulness'. When we face it with eyes front, it vanishes like an apparition. We may not all evolve that type of courage. But I am certain that Swaraj is unattainable this year if some of us have not the courage which enables us to stand firm like a rock without retaliating. The might of the tyrant recoils upon himself when it meets with no response, even as an arm violently waved in the air suffers dislocation.
>
> — M. K. Gandhi : *Young India*, October 26, 1921.

Just as violence should be negotiated by the inherent moral force to willingly die for humanism, so Truth and non-violence should form an integral part to usher forth desirable social consciousness. Gandhi applies and directs to apply non-violence to react against social ills primarily because it is the only living force that has its affinity to human welfare. As a matter of fact, to try to find out the inherent possibilities of Satyagraha as a great social force for transcendence is unending but thrilling. The greater the enquiry and observation for this purpose, the greater is the outcome for social and humanistic awareness. As Gandhi characteristically elucidates,

> Truth and *ahimsa* must incarnate in socialism. In order that they can, the votary must have a living faith in God. Mere mechanical adherence to truth and *ahimsa* is likely to break down at the critical moment. Hence have I said that truth is God. This God is a living Force. . . . That Force resides in, but is not the body. He who denies the existence of that great Force, denies to himself the use of that inexhaustible power and thus remains impotant. He is like a rudderless ship which, tossed about here and there, perishes without making any headway. The socialism of such takes them nowhere, what to say of the society in which they live.
>
> The fact is that it has always been a matter of strenuous research to this great Force and its hidden possibilities.
>
> — M. K. Gandhi : *Harijan*, July 20, 1947.

He also humbly adds,

> My claim is that in the pursuit of that search lies the discovery of *Satyagraha*. It is not, however, claimed that all the laws of *Satyagraha* have been laid down or found. This I do say, fearlessly and firmly, that every worthy object can be achieved by the use of *Satyagraha*. It is the highest and infallible means, the greatest force. Socialism will not be reached by any other means. Satyagraha can rid society of all evils, political, economic and moral.
>
> —*Ibid.*

To be a follower of Gandhian non-violence is also to be a follower of the great message : "If any man will take away thy coat, let him have thy clock also". In fact, this great message of humanism of the sermon on the Mount always serves as a guideline for Gandhi's doctrine of non-violence. As he characteristically explains,

> To take what is required may be profitable; to have more given to you is highly likely to be a burden. To overload a stomach is to court slow death. . . . When you give more to a robber than he needs, you spring a surprise on him, you give him a shock although agreeable. He has not been used to it. Historical instances are on record to show that such non-violent conduct has produced a wholesome effect upon evil-doers. These acts cannot be done mechanically; they must come out of conviction and love or pity for the other man. Nor need you work out all the apparent implications of my answer. If you do, you will come across blind alleys. Suffice it to say that in the verse quoted by you Jesus put in a picturesque and telling manner the great doctrine of non-violent non-cooperation. Your non-cooperation with your opponent is violent when you give a blow for a blow, and is ineffective in the long run. Your non-cooperation is non-violent when you give your opponent all in the place of just what he needs. You have disarmed him once for all by your apparent co-operation, which in effect is complete non-co-operation.
>
> — M. K. Gandhi : *Harijan*, July 13, 1940.

Non-violence that stands for conscious suffering for the awakening of true humanism has its added advantage. It is never static but always dynamic in the sense that it has a positive goal towards the march of humanism. Gandhi, therefore, advocates non-violence to understand and feel the inner strength of negotiating all evil forces that destroy humanism. In fact, his religion is the religion of humanism — the religion of the victory of man, that transcends everywhere. As he says,

> Non-violence in its dynamic condition means conscious suffering. It does not mean meek submission to the will of the evil-doer, but it means putting of one's whole soul against the will of the tyrant. Working under the law of our being, it is possible for a single individual to defy the whole might of an unjust empire to save his honour, his religion, his soul, and lay the foundation for that

> empire's fall or its regeneration.
>
> And so I am not pleading for India to practise non-violence because it is weak. I want her to practise non-violence being conscious of her strength and power. No training in arms is required for realisation of her strength. We seem to need it, because we seem to think that we are but a lump of flesh. I want to recognise that she has a soul that cannot perish and that can rise triumphant above every physical weakness and defy the physical combination of a whole world. . . . If India takes up the doctrine of the sword, she may gain momentary victory. Then India will cease to be the pride of my heart. I am wedded to India because I owe my all to her. I believe absolutely that she has a mission for the world. She is not to copy Europe blindly. India's acceptance of the doctrine of the sword will be the hour of my trial. I hope I shall not be found wanting.
>
> — D. G. Tendulkar : *Mahatma*, Publications Division, Ministry of Information and Broadcasting, Government of India Vol. II, pp. 5-6.

The lesson of Gandhian non-violence is one of natural humanism. It is the lesson that teaches mankind of oneness, the great truth of inseparable identity and also of the fact that all men and women are 'children of the same God'. One cannot, in this connection, but recall his poignant words against the proposed partition of India :

> As a man of non-violence, I cannot forcibly resist the proposed partition, if the Muslims of India really insist upon it. But, I never can be a willing party to the vivisection. I would employ every non-violent means to prevent it. For it means the undoing of centuries of work done by numberless Hindus and Muslims to live together as one nation. Partition means a patent untruth. My whole soul rebels against the idea that Hinduism and Islam represent two antagonistic cultures and doctrines. To assent to such a doctrine is for me denial of God. For I believe with my whole soul that the God of the Koran is also the God of the Gita, and that we are all, no matter by what name designated, children of the same God. I must rebel against the idea that Muslims or Indians who were Hindus the other day changed their nationality on adopting Islam as their religion.
>
> But that is my belief. I cannot thrust it down the throats of the

> Muslims who think that they are a different nation. I refuse, however, to believe that the Eight Crores of Muslims will say that they have nothing in common with their Hindu and other brethren. Their mind can only be known by a referendum made to them duly on that clear issue. The contemplated constituent assembly can easily decide the question. Naturally on an issue such as this, there can be no arbitration. It is purely a matter of self-determination. I know of no other conclusive method of ascertaining the mind of the Eight Crores of Muslims.
>
> D. G. Tendulkar : *Mahatma,* Publications Division, Ministry of Information and Broadcasting, Government of India, Vol. V, p. 271.

Humanism in the Gandhian and true concept cannot compromise with narrowness. It cannot make room for individual or narrow self-interest. It must allow wider contemplation for mankind. The history of an advanced and civilised world is the history of refined humanism. Gandhi advocates for that type of refined humanism which never allows narrowness to creep in the mind of mankind and destroy all good sense and sensibilities for the common cause of peace and prosperity. Co-ordination and consolidation of national and global culture, harmonisation of the inner spirit and enquiry of man and an endless pursuit for the all-round welfare of humanity — all these await, in Gandhian concept of humanism, a re-thinking in right earnest right now for our furtherance of cosmopolitan and global outlook. Gandhi's own humanistic outlook is a true source of humanism for the posterity :

> I cannot think in terms of narrow Hinduism or narrow Islam. I am wholly uninterested in a patchwork solution. India is a big country, a big nation composed of different cultures, which are tending to blend with one another, each complementing the rest. If I must wait for the completion of the process, I must wait. It may not be completed in my day. I shall love to die in the faith that it must come in the fullness of time. I should be happy to think that I had done nothing to hamper the process. And subject to this condition, I would do anything to bring about harmony. My life is made up of compromises, but they have been compromises that have brought me nearer the goal.
>
> —*Ibid.*, p. 273.

Explaining further on the power of non-violence, Gandhi predicts that the future of non-violence also determines the future of humanism. The potency of non-violence depends on how individuals dedicate themselves for the cause of humanism by means of adopting non-violence in every walk of life. If all individuals are greatly conscious of the role of non-violence for the progress of mankind, even a Nero cannot but revive the silent and dormant spirit of humanism within him. As Gandhi observes,

> I believe that a State can be administered on a non-violent basis if the vast majority of the people are non-violent. So far as I know, India is the only country which has a possibility of being such a State. I am conducting my experience in that faith. Supposing, therefore, that India attained independence through pure non-violence. India could retain it too by the same means. A non-violent man of society does not anticipate or provide for attacks from without. On the contrary, such a person of society firmly believes that nobody is going to disturb them. If the worst happens, there are two ways open to non-violence. To yield possession but non-cooperate with the aggressor. Thus, supposing that a modern edition of Nero descended upon India, the representatives of the State will let him in but tell him that he will get no assistance from the people. They will prefer death to submission. The second way would be non-violent resistance by the people who have been trained in the non-violent way. They would offer themselves unarmed as fodder for the aggressor's cannon. The underlying belief in either case is that even a Nero is not devoid of a heart. The unexpected spectacle of endless rows upon rows of men and women simply dying rather than surrender to the will of an aggressor must ultimately melt him and his soldiery. Practically speaking there will probably be no greater loss in men than if forcible resistance is offered; there will be no expenditure in armaments and fortification. The non-violent training received by the people will add inconceivably to their moral height.
>
> — M. K. Gandhi : *Harijan*, April 13, 1940.

What would be the lot of people practised in non-violent resistance before gun-point ? Would it be an act of mere chivalry or moral victory? As a sentinel of humanism, Gandhi believes that bravery, in the true sense of the term, lies in dying and not in killing. It also lies in upholding and maintaining the spirit of love rather than that of hatred. As non-violence knows no defeat, man thrives and voices the spirit of humanism from time-to-time. The true men and women followers of non-violence proclaim the eternal joy of life in love rather than in hate:

> Such men and women will have shown personal bravery of a type far superior to that shown in armed warfare. In each case the bravery consists in dying, not in killing. Lastly, there is no such thing as defeat in non-violent resistance. That such a thing has not happened before is no answer to my speculation. I have drawn no impossible picture. History is replete with instances of individual non-violence of the type I have mentioned. There is no warrant for saying or thinking that a group of men and women cannot by sufficient training act non-violently as a group or nation. Indeed the sumtotal of the experience of mankind is that men somehow or other live on. From which fact I infer that it is the law of love that rules mankind. Had violence, i.e. hate, ruled us, we should have become extinct long ago. And yet the tragedy of it is that the so-called civilised men and nations conduct themselves as if the basis of society was violence. It gives me ineffable joy to make experiments proving that love is the supreme and only law of life. Much evidence to the contrary cannot shake my faith. Even the mixed non-violence of India has supported it. But if it is not enough to convince an unbeliever, it is enough to incline a friendly critic to view it with favour.
>
> —*Ibid.*

The strength of mankind is, as Gandhi emphasises, one of self-defence that also characterises the superiority of man to other living objects of nature. Self-defence as one of the strategies of non-violence heightens humanism to the extent of self-sacrifice heroically or in its purity of form that necessitates such practice in courage and compassion. The strength of self-defence is thus enlightened with the halo of efflorescence rather than with the pale thought of extinction of mankind :

> The strength to kill is not essential for self-defence; one ought to have the strength to die when a man is fully ready to die, he will not even desire to offer violence. Indeed, I may put it down as a self-evident proposition that the desire to kill is in inverse proportion to the desire to die. And history is replete with instances of men who by dying with courage and compassion on their lips converted the hearts of their violent opponents.
>
> — R. K. Prabhu & U. R. Rao : *The Mind of Mahatma Gandhi*, Oxford University Press, 1945, pp. 48-49.

As a foreseer of humanism, Gandhi believes that the future of humanity depends on eliminating hatred against the down-trodden and the deprived, the weak and the mute millions who never bother for force or the wistful outcome of force. The dignity of human beings is to be nursed not with violence of hatred but with mutual love and sympathy. From his own rich experience of harmonisation of a global society in the frame-work of non-violence, he observes :

> The accumulated experience of the past thirty years, the first eight of which were in South Africa, fills me with the greatest hope that in the adoption of non-violence lies the future of India and the world. It is the most harmless and yet equally effective way of dealing with the political and economic wrongs of the down-trodden portion of humanity. I have known from early youth that non-violence is not a cloistered virtue to be practised by the individual for the peace and final salvation, but it is a rule of conduct for society if it is to live consistently with human dignity and make progress towards the attainment of peace for which it has been yearning for ages past.
>
> — M. K. Gandhi : *Gandhiji's Correspondence with the Government*, 1942-44, Navajivan Publishing House, Ahmedabad, 1945, p. 170.

To wish ill to anybody or show hatred by any means, therefore, mars the victory of humanism paved through non-violence. A constant effort at non-attachment makes anyone equipped with the realisation of himself to the fullest extent — the realisation of God, indeed, who is within himself. Such an extent of human endeavour flashes Truth and merges it to non-violence. Gandhi's own elucidation highlights the point better :

> *Ahimsa* is not the crude thing it has been made to appear. Not to hurt any living thing is no doubt a part of *ahimsa*. But it is its least expression. The principle of *ahimsa* is hurt by every evil thought, by undue haste, by living, by hatred, by wishing ill to anybody. It is also violated by our holding on to what the world needs. But the world needs even what we eat day by day. In the place where we stand there are millions of micro organisms to whom the place belongs and who are hurt by our presence there. What should we do then ? Should we commit suicide ? Even that is no solution, if we believe, as we do, that so long as the spirit is attached to the flesh, on every destruction of the body it weaves for itself another. The body will cease to be only when we give up all attachment to it. This freedom from all attachment is the realisation of God as truth. Such realisation cannot be attained in a hurry. The body does not belong to us. When it lasts, we must use it as a trust handed over to our charge. Treating in this way, the things of the flesh, we may one day expect to become free from the burden of the body. Realising the limitations of the flesh, we must strive day by day towards the ideal with what strength we have in us.
>
> — M. K. Gandhi : *From Yeravda Mandir*. Navajivan Press, Ahmedabad, 1935, Chapter II, p. 31.

The emancipation of humanism in each individual through non-violence awaits release from all sensualities and striving for Truth. Indeed, truth and non-violence are so intertwined that in course of operation they lose separate identities and act as complementary to each other towards fulness of humanism. This fulness of humanism is the end-point of *ahimsa* that serves as a means of that end-point. Gandhi, therefore, visualises *ahimsa* as a means, and Truth the final victory of humanism. As he concludes.

> *Ahimsa* and Truth are so intertwined that it is practically impossible to disentangle and separate them. They are like the two sides of a coin, or rather of a smooth unstamped metallic disc. Who can say, which is the obverse and which is the

> reverse? Nevertheless *ahimsa* is the means, Truth is the end. Means to be means must always be within our reach, and so *ahimsa* is our supreme duty. If we take care of the means, we are bound to reach the end sooner of later. When once we have grasped this point, final victory is beyond question. Whatever apparent reverses we sustain, we may not give up the quest for Truth which alone is, being God himself.
>
> —*Ibid.*

That the education of *satyagraha* is the education of perfection, the education that excels humanism is the most remarkable contribution for which Gandhi will ever remain illustrious in the history of human advancement. What he essentially emphasises is to inspire emancipation of the greater self in everyone from his little self—an emancipation that calls forth awakening and exercise of the soul-force. This necessitates a prolonged training in disinterested service towards mankind. Such a training will enable everyone to be perfect and pure, although it admits the fact that perfection or purity of an individual is an unending process. But the education of non-violence even exceeds and excels the best education received from anywhere. This is the education that prepares everyone to be equipped with the weapons of love, truth and self-suffering for the cause of humanism. Gandhi delineates this fact very adroitly :

> All *Satyagrahis* do not understand the full value of the force, nor have we men who always from conviction refrain from violence. The use of this force requires the adoption of poverty, in the sense that we must be indifferent whether we have the wherewithal to feed or clothe ourselves. During the past struggle all *Satyagrahis*, if any at all, were not prepared to go that length. So again were only *Satyagrahis* so-called. They came without any conviction, often with mixed motives, less often with impure motives. Some even, whilst engaged in the struggle, would gladly have resorted to violence but for most vigilant supervision. Thus, it was that the struggle became prolonged; for the exercise of the purest soul-force, in its perfect form, brings about instantaneous relief. For this exercise, prolonged training of the individual soul is an absolute necessity, so that a perfect *Satyagrahi* has to be almost, if not entirely, a perfect man. We cannot all suddenly become

such men, but if my proposition is correct — as a I know it to be correct — the greater the spirit of Satyagraha in us, the better men will we become.

— M. K. Gandhi : *Young India,* November 3, 1927.

For evolution of better humanism, Gandhi, therefore, wants to incorporate the education of *Satyagraha* — the education of perfect living — in the education of the child, keeping in view the dedicated personalities to humanism :

If the past struggle has produced even a few Indians who would dedicate themselves to the task of becoming *Satyagrahis* as nearly perfect as possible, they would not only have served themselves in the truest sense of the term, they would also have served humanity at large. Thus viewed, *Satyagraha* is the noblest and best education. It should come, not after the ordinary education in letters, of children, but it should precede it. It will not be denied, that a child, before it begins to write its alphabet and to gain worldly knowledge, should know what the soul is, what truth is, what love is, what powers are latent in the soul. It should be an essential part of real education that a child should learn, that in the struggle of life, it can easily conquer hate by love, untruth by truth, violence by self-suffering.

— *Ibid.*

Even when he introduces the spinning wheel as an invaluable apparatus for self-understanding, self-economy, self-respect and self-dependence, Gandhi symbolises it as the non-violent approach to humanism. Conversion of the oppressor can only be made peacefully and poignantly by means of introducing the spinning wheel — a weapon of self-consciousness and self-defence. While negotiating a challenge from a speaker in the open Congress Session in connection with detachment of the *Charkha* from *Satyagraha*, Gandhi's emphatic reply is :

Well, I tell you, as I have been telling you these 20 years, that there is a vital connection between *Satyagraha* and the *Charkha*, and the more I find that belief challenged the more I am confined

> in it. Otherwise I am no fool to persist in turning the *Charkha*, day in and day out, at home and even on trains, in the teeth of medical advice. I want you too to be turning the *Charkha* with the same faith. And unless you do it and unless you habitually use *Khadi* you will deceive me and deceive the world.
>
> — M. K. Gandhi : *Harijan*, March 30, 1940.

Relating further on his loyalty to the *Charkha* that also contributes a great deal to the success at *Satyagraha* and for that end in view of humanism, Gandhi adds :

> I know that you will not fight unless you have me with you, but then you must know that I am here and I would fight only as a representative of those dumb millions for whom I live and for whom I want to die. My loyalty to them is greater than any other loyalty, and it is for them that I would not give up the *Charkha* even if you were to forsake me or kill me. . . . The *Charkha* is an outward symbol of truth and non-violence, and unless you have them in your hearts you will not take to the *Charkha* either. Remember, therefore, that you have to fulfil both the internal and external conditions. If you fulfil the internal condition, you will cease to hate your opponent, you will not seek or work for his destruction, but pray to God to have mercy on him. Do not, therefore, concentrate on showing the misdeeds of the Government, for we have to convert and befriend those who run it. And after all no one is wicked by nature. And if others are wicked, are we the less so ? The attitude is interest in Satyagraha, and if you do not subscribe to it, even then I would ask you to leave me.
>
> —*Ibid.*

Suffering unto death as sponsored by Gandhian *Satyagraha* is the last weapon of revival of true humanism and victory of Truth. As an element of *Satyagraha* fasting takes a very important role for awakening of good sense and sensibilities. If symbolises complete physical detachment and deep devotion to the cause of humanism. After a 21-day observance of fast for the cause of the Harijan in May 1933, Gandhi writes :

> The fast was an uninterrupted twenty-one days' prayer whose effect I can feel even now. I know now more fully than ever that there is no prayer without fasting, be the latter were so little. And this fasting relates not merely to the palate, but all the senses and organs. Complete absorption in prayer must mean complete exclusion of physical activities till prayer possesses the work of our being and we rise superior to, and are completely detached from, all physical functions. The state can only be reached after continual and voluntary crucifixion of the flesh. Thus all fasting, if it is a spiritual act, is an intense prayer or a preparation for it. It is a yearning of the soul to merge in the divine essence.
>
> — M. K. Gandhi : *Harijan*, July 8, 1933.

Earlier, Gandhi explains why he should go on fasting as a humanistic endeavour to explore Truth through *ahimsa* :

> Suffering even unto death and, therefore, even through a perpetual fast is the last weapon of a Satyagrahi. That is the last duty which it is open to him to perform. Therefore, fast is part of my being as, I hold, it has been, to a large or small extent, of very seeker of truth. I am making an experiment in *ahimsa* on a scale perhaps unknown in history. That I may be wholly wrong is quite possible, but quite irrelevant to the present purpose. So long as I am not conscious of the error, but, on the contrary, am sure, as far as it is humanly possible to be, of being in the right, I must go on with my pursuit to the furthest end. And in this manner, but in no other, a fast or a series of fasts are always a possibility in my life. I have undergone many before now since childhood. There should be no alarm felt if they are undertaken for public causes. Nor must anyone exploit them in anticipation. When they come, they will produce their own effect and result, whether anybody wills or no.
>
> — M. K. Gandhi : *Harijan*, February 18, 1933.

The lesson of non-violence learnt through the Gandhian concept of humanism is that lesson of the inner soul that marks one's excellence as a human being. And that excellence is the excellence attained in Truth, self-negation and humility. When, as Gandhi believes, one wins over one's physical bare necessities, the dawn of humanism awakens in the midst of non-violence. As he elucidates,

> It is a fundamental principle of *Satyagraha* that the tyrant whom the Satyagrahi seeks to resist has power over his body and natural possessions but he can have no power over the soul. The soul can remain unconquered and unconquerable even when the body is imprisoned. The whole science of *Satyagraha* was born from a knowledge of this fundamental truth, . . . Nature's creatures do not worry or fret about tomorrow but simply wait on tomorrow for the daily sustenance. Only man is in his overweaning pride and egotism imagines himself to be the Lord and master of the earth, and goes on piling up for himself goods that perish. Nature frees away everyday by its rude shocks to wean him from his pride but he refuses to shed it. Satyagraha is a specific for bringing home to one the lesson of humanity.
>
> — M. K. Gandhi : *Young India*, May 21, 1931.

As an optimist, Gandhi believes in the endless possibilities of man in extending the horizons of humanism through non-violence. He also believes that on the threshold of a new era of consciousness, man will herald his own glory along with the glory of humanism. He will, through exercise of non-violence, eliminate this selfish attitudes and attractions for the little self and extend the doors and windows of awareness towards the march of humanism. The element of love, an essential component of non-violence and, for that end in view, humanism accelerates this march to build up the world anew. In the whirlwind of aggression and hatred loomed large on humanity, the Orphic voice of Gandhi necessitates a worthy re-hearing :

> I am an optimist. My optimism rests on my belief in the infinite possibilities of the individual to develop non-violence. The more you develop it in your own being, the more infectious it becomes till it overwhelms your surroundings and by and by might oversweep the world.
>
> — R. K. Prabhu & U. R. Rao : *The Mind of Mahatma Gandhi*, Oxford University Press, London, 1945, p. 46.

Do we really listen to the Orphic voice for the march of humanism?

7

THE HUMANISTIC APPROACH TO EDUCATION : Gandhian Viewpoints

EDUCATION, AS Gandhi believes, is what man should be form what he is. It is a vehicle of his transcendence and, at the same time, it is a means of evolution of human consciousness. Man excels all other animals because he alone has the capacity to be christened with the beyonding of consciousness. Man excels all living beings because he has an added quality to remodel his own vision and imagination for the welfare of one and all. Man excels because he has the insatiable spirit of adventure within him — the spirit that knows no defeat.

Gandhi voices the spirit of victory in man — the victory that is achieved through the right type of education that prepares a right mind to go ahead in the right direction towards fulness and beyonding. The victory that such type of education brings forth is also based on a sound platform of moral, aesthetic, religious and spiritual upliftment. For a right mind crystallised in appropriate education, Gandhi advocates for purity of thought and action right from early childhood, for he thinks that the birth of man signifies a holy grail — rebirth of All Beautiful in efflorescence. For such a pure and holy birth of man, he emphasises a great deal on the education of the heart which, as he believes, cannot be imparted by so-called bookish education. He, therefore, suggests on the importance of teachers who are ethically and aesthetically sound in taking up the arduous task of turning out pupils as worthy living citizens of tomorrow. Gandhi's realistic observations are :

> I do not believe that this (the education of the heart) can be imparted through books. It can only be done through the living touch of the teacher. And who are the teachers in the primary and even secondary schools? Are they men and women of faith and

> character? Have they themselves received the training of the heart? Are they ever expected to take care of the permanent element in the boys and girls placed under their charge? Is not the method of engaging teachers for lower schools an effective bar against character? . . . And we know, that the teachers of primary schools are not selected for their patriotism.
>
> – M.K. Gandhi : *Young India*, September, 1921.

Education thus ill-directed *sans* humanitarian and patriotic ends in view fails to serve the real purpose. It also fails to draw the best out of man. As Gandhi strongly remarks :

> Real education consists in drawing the best out of yourself. What better book can there be than the book of humanity?
>
> – M.K. Gandhi : *Harijan*, March 30, 1934.

Like an iconoclast in educational reforms, Gandhi spells out the fundamental objectives of education from practical aspects of life. He wants education — and rightly so — to be dynamic, living and, above all, humanistic. According to him, it is, therefore, better not to have any education detached from life than to have it in the form of stereotyped, patchy, sterile grasping of reading, writing and arithmetic *sans* meaning *sans* usability. Mere apeing of Western strategies in the arena of education might mechanically boost us towards so-called progressivism but this would hardly contribute towards advancement of humanism. As Gandhi gravely observes:

> To teach boys reading, writing and arithmetic is called primary education. A peasant earns his bread honestly. He has ordinary knowledge of the world. He knows fairly well how he should behave towards his parents, his wife, his children and his fellow-villagers. He understands and observes the rules of morality. But he cannot write his own name. What do you propose to do by giving him a knowledge of letters? Will you add an inch to his happiness? Do you wish to make him discontested with his cottage or his lot? And even if you want to do that, he will not need such an education. Carried away by the flood of Western thought, we came to the conclusion, without weighing pros and cons, that we should

give this kind of education to the people.

– M.K. Gandhi : *Young India*, June 1, 1921.

Training in conscience, tender and sensitive and forming an essential component in humanistic education is, let us frankly admit, yet a far cry. Quite ahead of professional thinkers and innovators in education, Gandhi evaluates higher education from the standpoint of Huxleyan concept of education as an invaluable means for accelerating humanism and bewails the lot of so-called higher education in case of none else than his own one :

> I have learned Geography, Astronomy, Algebra, Geometry, etc. What of that? In what way have I benefitted myself or these around me? Why have I learned these things? Professor Huxley has thus defined education :
>
> > 'That man I think has had a liberal education who has been so trained in youth that his body is the ready servant of his will and does with ease and pleasure all the work that as a mechanism it is capable of; whose intellect is a clear, cold, logic engine with all its parts of equal strength and in smooth working order . . . whose mind is stored with a knowledge of the fundamental truths of nature whose passions are trained to come to heel by a vigorous will, the servant of a tender conscience . . . who has learnt to hate all vileness and to respect others as himself. Such a one and no other, I conceive, has had a liberal education, for he is in harmony with Nature. He will make the best of her and she of him.'
>
> If this be true education, I must emphatically say that the sciences I have enumerated above I have never been able to use for controlling my senses. Therefore, whether you take elementary education or higher education, it is not required for the main thing. It does not make of us men. It does not enable us to do our duty.

– *Ibid.*

Whatever education we receive does not corporate with our real living, real having and real being. Revival of the ancient system of education as Gandhi desires, takes a major role in character-building that also builds the solid Foundation of humanism. This is what liberal education should aim at and this is what mechanised education fights shy of. When education shines in use it serves its purpose best like shining ornaments. Gandhi's own elucidation is noteworthy :

> I have not run down a knowledge of letters under all circumstances. All I have shown is that we must not make of it a fetish. It is not our *Kamadhuk*. In its place it can be of use and it has its place when we have brought our senses under subjection, and put our ethics on a firm foundation. And then, if we feel inclined to receive that education, we may make good use of it. As an ornament it is likely to sit well on us. It now follows that it is not necessary to make this education compulsory. Our ancient school system is enough. Character-building has the first place in it, and that is primary education. A building erected on that foundation will last.
>
> –*Ibid.*

Even in case of development of intelligence, Gandhi negates the value of book-reading for he firmly believes that education dissociated from the quickest development of the mind by means of real life experience through manual excellence is devoid of humanistic appeal. A real harmony of education and employment is possible when education is liberalised to the extent of sharing mutual experiences and aspirations for the welfare of mankind. As Gandhi categorically states :

> The utterly false idea that intelligence can be developed only through book-reading should give place to the truth that the quickest development of the mind can be achieved by artisan's work being learnt in a scientific manner. True development of the mind commences immediately the apprentice is taught at every step why a particular manipulation of the hand or a tool is required. The problem of the unemployment of students can be solved without difficulty, if they will rank themselves among the common labourers.
>
> – M.K. Gandhi : *Harijan*, January 9, 1937.

An unusually exceptional radical humanist, Gandhi brings education down to the level of ordinary labourers when systematisation in education for the sake of compartmentalisation and, for a great extent, alienation passes through agonised moments of establishment. He also brings down conservation in education to highlight the fact that true education is always an emancipation — *Sa vidya ya vimuktaye* (an inner awakening to be worthy of oneself in order to be worthy of all). When he thinks of the education of children, he primarily lends importance to 'an all-round drawing of the best' for humanism. The teaching of useful handicrafts for which he advocated will pave avenues for having that type of humanistic education which will enable the learner to have an all-round development in him of body, mind and spirit. Education for humanisation is, therefore, the primary need on which Gandhi harps again and again. Here is his practical approach to education for development of humanism :

> By education I mean an all-round drawing out of the best in child and man — body, mind and spirit. Literacy is not the end of education nor even the beginning. It is only one of the means whereby man and woman can be educated. Literacy in itself is no education. I would therefore begin the child's education by teaching it a useful handicraft and enabling it to produce from the moment it begins its training. Thus every school can be made self-supporting, the condition being that the state takes over the manufactures of these schools.
>
> I hold that the highest development of the mind and the soul is possible under such a system of education. Only every handicraft has to be taught not merely mechanically as is done today but scientifically, i.e. the child should know the why and the wherefore of every process. I am not writing this without some confidence, because it has the backing of experience. This method is being adopted more or less completely wherever spinning is being taught to workers. I have myself taught sandal-making and even spinning on these lines with good results. This method does not exclude a knowledge of history and geography. But I find that this is best taught by transmitting such general information by word or mouth. One imparts ten times as much in this manner as by reading and writing. The signs of the alphabet may be taught later when the pupil has learnt to distinguish wheat from chaff and when he has somewhat developed his or her tastes. This is a revolutionary proposal but it saves immense labour and enables a student to acquire in one year what he may take much longer to learn. This

means all-round economy. Of course the pupil learns mathematics whilst he is learning his handicraft.

– M.K. Gandhi : *Harijan*, July 31, 1937.

Education for awakening of self-consciousness to foster humanism awaits an indepth study of natural behavioural design of the human species. Gandhi starts his experiment on education for efflorescence of humanism from this broad perspective that caters to natural and desirable human growth and development. He, therefore, emphasises on education as a total involvement of life from all dimensions — physical, social, economic, cultural, aesthetic, religious and spiritual — so that all the humane sensibilities might be allowed to fillip inherent human potentiality and spontaneity. Even in the education of women he desires to have this human development at par with men, for he believes that education is always a worthy vehicle for emancipation of humanism. In a speech delivered on February 20, 1918, he observes:

> I have never placed an unnecessarily high value on the knowledge of the three R's. I am only attempting to assign its proper place to it. I have pointed out from time to time that there is no justification for men to deprive women of, or to deny to them, equal rights on the ground of their illiteracy. But education is essential for enabling women to assert these natural rights, to exercise them wisely, and to work for their expansion; again, the true knowledge of self is unattainable by the millions who lack such education. Many a book is full of innocent pleasure, and this will be denied to us without education. It is no exaggeration to say that human being without education is not far removed from an animal. Education, therefore, is necessary for women as it is for men.

– M.K. Gandhi : *Women and Social Justice*, Navajivan Publishing House, Ahmedabad, 1945, p. 3.

For a common endeavour in exposing the greatness of the inner being, Gandhi's vision of humanism as reflected through his educational plans and programmes for women also reflects a certain sense of aesthetic consciousness. In fact, the aesthetics of non-violence can be best expanded by means of extending leadership to women who might propagate the lesson of humanism in every walk of life. This will also eliminate all sorts of inferiority complex from which women even now suffer. Moreover, with equal approach to the field of the march for humanism, the sex instincts and impulses of human behaviour will be to a great extent eliminated. The new aura of consciousness for furtherance of humanism will have its solid foundation on education for better efflorescence. Gandhi explains the point quite characteristically :

> The division of the spheres of work being recognised, the general qualities and culture required are practically the same for both the sexes.
>
> My contribution to the great problem lies in my presenting for acceptance truth and *ahimsa* in every walk of life, whether for individuals or nations. I have hugged the hope that in this woman will be the unquestionable leader and, having thus found her place in human evolution, she will shed her inferiority complex. If she is able to do this successfully she must resolutely refuse to believe in the modern teaching that everything is determined and regulated by the sex impulse. I fear I have put the proposition rather clumsily. But I hope my meaning is clear. I do not know that the millions of men who are taking an active part in the war are obsessed by the sex spectre. Nor are the peasants working together in their fields worried or dominated by it. This is not to say or suggest that they are free from the instinct implanted in man and woman. But it most certainly does not dominate their lives as it seems to dominate the lives of those who are saturated with the modern sex literature. Neither man nor woman has time for such things when he or she is faced with the hard fact of living life in its grim reality.
>
> — M.K. Gandhi : *Harijan*, February 24, 1940.

The education of women for dissemination of humanism has its other aspects, too. For Gandhi, education is never detached from reality. And, for that end in view, he derides on any approach that snatches away a woman from her hearth, tears apart the bond of love and affection, uproots motherliness and, instead, places the rifle on her hands to stamp mockeries in the name of humanism. The education for awareness to humane sensibilities cannot but begin from home where women teach the lesson of harmony of human behaviour. The education of looking in reverence for women, as Gandhi feels, fosters humanism towards nobler direction. Notwithstanding the apparent equality of man and woman, he, therefore, highlights woman from a new angle of radical humanism :

> My own opinion is that, just as fundamentally men and women are one, their problem must be one in essence. The soul in both is the same. The two live the same life, have the same feelings. Each is a complement of the other. The one cannot live without the other's active help.
>
> But somehow or other man has dominated woman from ages past, and so woman has developed an inferiority complex. She has believed in the truth of man's interested teaching that she is inferior to him.
>
> — M. K. Gandhi : *Harijan*, February 24, 1940.

To eliminate the coercive teaching of man's supremacy over woman, Gandhi thinks that education has a great role to bring woman to the forefront of human development and human civilisation. In fact, the humanistic approach to education to the above end in view opens a new chapter on Gandhian humanism for the future. As he argues,

> Nevertheless there is no doubt that at some point there is bifurcation. Whilst both are fundamentally one, it is also equally true that in the form there is a vital difference between the two. Hence the vocations of the two must also be different. The duty of motherhood, which the vast majority of women will always undertake, requires qualities which man need not possess. She is passive, he is active. She is essentially mistress of the house. He is the bread-winner. She is the keeper and distributor of the bread. She is the care-taker in every sense of the term. The art of bringing up the infants of the race is her special and sole prerogative. Without her care, the race must become extinct.
>
> —*Ibid.*

Highlighting the above views on the core of humanism, Gandhi broadens the spectrum of the role of women for educating men with softer sensibilities of humanism through orderliness, calmness, tolerance and numerous other humane sensibilities thoroughly and efficiently :

> In my opinion, it is degrading both for man and woman that woman should be called upon or induced to forsake the hearth and shoulder the rifle for the protection of that hearth. It is a reversion to barbarity and the beginning of the end. In trying to ride the horse that man rides, she brings herself and him down. The sin will be on man's head for tempting or compelling his companion to desert her special calling. There is as much bravery in keeping one's home in good order and condition as there is in defending it against attack from without.
>
> —*Ibid.*

Perhaps from this wide spectrum of living humanism Gandhi gives a great deal of emphasis on the education of tolerance. The lesson of tolerance is the lesson of inwardness, of clarity of vision and humanism. It allows the learner to control impatience and nursle magnanimity of mind. It allows the mind to endure and observe, defend and restore Truth at all costs. In this connection, Gandhi's reaction to *dharna* is remarkable :

> Some students have revived the ancient form of barbarity in the form of 'sitting *dharna*'. I call it 'barbarity' for it is a crude way of using coercion. It is also cowardly because one who 'sits dharna' knows he is not going to be trampled over. It is difficult to call the practice violence, but it is certainly worse. If we fight our opponent, we at least enable him to return the blow. But when we challenge him to walk over us, we, *knowing* that he will not, place him in a most awkward and humiliating position. I know that the overzealous students who 'sat *dharna*' never thought of the barbarity of the deed. But one, who is expected to follow the voice of conscience and stand even single-handed in the face of odds, cannot afford to be thoughtless. Non-co-operation, if it fails, will fail only through internal weakness. There is no such thing as defeat in non-co-operation. It never fails. Its so-called representatives may so badly represent their cause that it may appear to the spectators to have failed. Let non-co-operationists therefore beware of everything they do. There must be no

impatience, no barbarity, no insolence, no undue pressure. If we want to cultivate a true spirit of democracy, we cannot afford to be intolerant. Intolerance betrays want of faith in one's cause.

— M. K. Gandhi : *Young India*, February 2, 1921.

For introducing a 'whole education' that encompasses humanism, Gandhi greatly feels that it should impart pupils a training in some craft or industry. This will enable them to grow up both intellectually and humanely. For this, living and practical education, keeping in view the needs of the greater human society, must be given a priority. As the society needs an ideal human development, education cannot but be an organ of education for humanism. As Gandhi frankly states,

> I want that the whole education should be imparted through some handicraft or industry. It might be objected that in the middle ages only handicrafts were taught to the students; but the occupational training, then, was far from serving an educational purpose. The crafts were taught only for sake of the crafts, without any attempt to develop the intellect as well. In this age those born to certain professions had forgotten them, had taken to clerical careers and were lost to country side. The remedy lies in imparting the whole art and science of a craft through practical training and there-through imparting the whole education.

— M. K. Gandhi : *Harijan*, October 30, 1937.

Gandhi goes so far as to orient the whole system of education on self-dependence and austerity. He even synchronises education and economy and extends the humanistic approach to education from a broad-based blue-print of objectives :

> I am very keen on finding the expenses of a teacher through the product of the manual work of his pupils, because I am convinced that there is no other way to carry education to crores of our children. . . . The present generation of boys know no cleanliness, no self-help, and are physically weak. I would, therefore, give compulsory physical training through musical drill.

— *Ibid.*

In this connection, one might recall Gandhi's crusade against dehumanised education in the boycott of schools that turn out only future clerks and eat up pupils' moral and humanistic outlook. Since sharing the responsibilities of a country's freedom is greater than nursing indolence that grows cancerously under the yoke of foreign dominance, Gandhi proposes for boycotting schools that patronise debased humanism. As he observes,

> I feel that if we do not have the courage to suspend the education of our children, we do not deserve to win the battle.
>
> I contend that there is no sacrifice involved in emptying the schools. We must be specially unfit for non-co-operation if we are so helpless as to be unable to manage our own education in total independence of the Government. Every village should manage the education of its own children. I would not depend upon Government aid. If there is a real awakening the schooling need not be interrupted for a single day. The very school masters who are now conducting Government schools, if they are good enough to resign their office, could take charge of national schools and teach our children the things they need, and not make of the majority of them indifferent clerks. I do look to the Aligarh college to give the lead in this matter. The moral effect created by the emptying of our *madrasas* will be tremendous.
>
> * * * *
>
> Indeed, what could be grander education than that the parents and scholars should put religious sentiment before a knowledge of letters ? If therefore no arrangement could be immediately made for the literary instruction of youths who might be withdrawn, it would be most profitable training for them to be able to work as volunteers for the cause which may necessitate their withdrawal from Government schools. For as in the case of the lawyers, so in the case of boys, my notion of withdrawal does not mean an indolent life. The withdrawing boys will, each according to his worth, be expected to take this share in the agitation.
>
> — M. K. Gandhi : *Young India*, August, 1920.

Like a revolutionary humanist in educational reorientation, Gandhi visualises the urgent need of implementing some basic drafts to eliminate appalling differences among pupils in urban and rural schools. Urban exploitation in the name of education and economy — who ignores ? — still persists. Gandhi makes a realistic approach to education suggesting means for averting alienation between rural and urban life. For this, social reconstruction takes a prominent part in extending programmes of education for revival of crafts. A direct channellised and effective programme of vocational education as he suggests might avert human wastage, undesirable dependence on mechanical power and materials and restore the care of humanism among mankind everywhere. Upholding the cause of humanism, he makes vocationalisation of education in rural areas a priority :

> I want to resuscitate the villages of India. Today our villages have become a mere appendage to the cities. They exist, as it were, to be exploited by the latter and depend on the latter's sufferance. This is unnatural. It is only when the cities realise the duty of making an adequate return to the villages for the strength and sustenance which they derive from them, instead of selfishly exploiting them, that a healthy and moral relationship between the two will spring up. And if the city children are to play their part in this great and noble work of social reconstruction, the vocations through which they are to achieve their education ought to be directly related to the requirements of the villages. So far as I can see, the various processes of cotton manufacture from ginning and clearing of cotton to the spinning of yarn, answer this test as nothing else does. Even today cotton is grown in the villages and is ginned and spun and converted into cloth in the cities. But the chain of processes which cotton undergoes in the mills from the beginning to the end constitutes a huge tragedy of waste in men, materials and mechanical power.
>
> — M. K. Gandhi : *Harijan*, October 9, 1937.

For a humanistic synchronisation between the rural and the urban masses, Gandhi's plan is, therefore, to launch the education of handicrafts like spinning, carding etc. that will serve as a great force for social re-orientation. Moreover, a certain sense of moral advancement is also possible by means of introducing education for humanism. Education, right from the primary stage, should, therefore, aim at simplicity through incorporation of handicrafts, which will also serve as a means for all-round national cohesion. As Gandhi elucidates,

> My plan to impart primary education through the medium of village handicrafts like spinning and carding, etc. is thus conceived as the spearhead of a silent social revolution fraught with the most far reaching consequences. It will provide a healthy and moral basis of relationship between the city and the village and thus go a long way towards eradicating some of the worst evils of the present social insecurity and poisoned relationship between the classes. It will check the progressive decay of our villages and lay the foundations of a juster social order in which there is no unnatural division between the 'haves' and the 'have-nots' and everybody is assured of a living wage and the right to freedom. And all this would be accomplished without the horror of a bloody class war or a colossal capital expenditure such as would be involved in the mechanisation of a vast continent like India.
>
> — M. K. Gandhi : *Harijan,* October 9, 1937.

As a humanist, Gandhi believes that freedom of mind rather than freedom from mere bondage is an essential outcome of education. Therefore, in educating children right from the early stage, ample scope should be provided for fulfilment of an individual pupil's endless curiosity. Freedom of expression and appreciation is a vital factor that greatly contributes to the development of humanism. As he suggests,

> As regards children's curiosity about the facts of life, we should tell them if we know, and admit our ignorance if we do not. If it is something that must not be told, we should check them and ask them not to put such questions even to anyone else. We must never put them off. They know more things than we imagine. If they do not know and if we refuse to tell them, they try to acquire the knowledge in a questionable manner. But if it has to be withheld from them, we must take such risk.
>
> — Mahadev Desai : *The Diary of Mahadev Desai,* Navajivan Publishing House, Ahmedabad, 1953, p. 188.

To allow freedom for children in education is to orient education in the humanistic pattern to enjoy and experience truth directly and consciously. This, indeed, broadens their mind and widens their outlook. As a matter of fact, to humanise education in the right perspective, Gandhi advocates for introduction of sex-education which, psychologically, is a surer way of 'conquest and sublimation of the sex passion':

> We cannot properly control, or conquer the sexual passion by turning a blind eye to it. I am, therefore, strongly in favour of teaching young boys and young girls the significance and right use of their generative organs. In my own way I have tried to impart this knowledge to young children of both sexes, for whose training I was responsible. But the sex education that I stand for must have for its object the sex passion. Such education should automatically serve to bring home to children the essential distinction between man and brute, to make them realise that it is man's privilege and pride to be gifted with the faculties of head and heart both, that he is a thinking no less than a feeling animal, and to renounce the sovereignty of reason over the blind instinct, is, therefore, to renounce a man's estate. In man reason quickens and guides the feeling, in brute the soul lies ever dormant. To awaken the heart is to awaken the dormant soul, to awaken reason and to inculcate discrimination between good and evil. Today, our entire environment — our reading, our thinking, and our social behaviour —is generally calculated to subserve and cater for the sex urge. To break through its coils is no easy task. But it is a task worthy of our highest endeavour.
>
> — D. G. Tendulkar : *Mahatma*, Publications Division, Ministry of Information and Broadcasting, Government of India. Vol. IV, p. 62.

Looking upon education as a means for awakening of the heart as well as of the soul instead of bare stuffing the brain with the complexities of reason and abstraction is what Gandhi considers to be the primary objective of education. For humanistic education, he, therefore, lays a great emphasis on manual labour that teaches one the invaluable qualities of self-dependence and self-respect. As he observes,

> The utterly false idea that intelligence can be developed only through book-reading should give place to the truth that the quickest development of the mind can be achieved by the artisan's work being learnt in a scientific manner. True development of the mind commences immediately the apprentice is taught at every step why a particular manipulation of the hand or a tool is required. The problem of the unemployment of students can be solved without difficulty, if they will rank themselves among the common labourers.
>
> — M. K. Gandhi : *Harijan*, January 9, 1937.

To ensure dignity in work is to ensure and promote humanism and to promote humanism is to consider work to be worship, act accordingly and receive the best out of education. With this practical and humanistic suggestivities in view, Gandhi wants to bring about a radical change in the concept of education. In fact, the basic idea of his basic education is :

> Work done with integrity and intelligence, is ultimately the only proper medium through which human beings can be truly educated and that schools must become active centres of 'doing' and 'learning by doing' both organised in integral relationship with each other. This appreciation of the intrinsic relationship between doing, learning and living is no accidental off-shoot, which Gandhiji's philosophy of life has put forth; it springs from the deepest sources of his thought. He has been a worker — and in contact with workers —throughout his life. He knows, through first-hand experience and observation, that all real value is created through honest work and that true culture is even more emphatically a product of the field, the farm and the workshop than of the library and the lectureroom.
>
> — K. G. Saiyidain : *Gandhiji : His Life and Work*, pp. 207-208.

What does Gandhi really want through basic education ? The answer, in short, is to deepen the inherent sense of humanity among children :

> He (Gandhi) aims at exalting co-operation above competition,

> service above exploitation, non-violence above violence. Above all, his educational scheme . . . is inspired by the hope that, by making all children learn co-operatively through craft work, thus sharing the life and labour of the masses, it will not release their productive powers for the service of the common good but deepen their sense of humanity and kinship with their fellowmen all over the world.
>
> —*Ibid.*, pp. 210-211.

When education is directed towards a growth within to embrace mankind from all avenues of excellence, it becomes a positive force of humanism. Gandhi appeals for that positive force.

That positive force alone can bring about the complete change in man — the change that Gandhi terms as re-education. For this a certain transformation of character and an elevation of personality are the two most desirable outcomes that form the basis of education. As Anibel del Campo observes,

> Gandhi advocated the complete transformation of men; and for this transformation, one of his important tools was education. He aimed at the re-education of character, and he sought to achieve this by giving them an ashramic or collective education. This last is one of the most important elements in Indian culture for the training of personality. Gandhi felt that by training the personality of men one would achieve a true revolution, since all revolutions are based on a transformation of education. That is why for Gandhi it was the core of the problem. The two elements which formed its base — truth and non-violence — always went together. It is only in their perspective that Gandhi saw the liberation of India. The liberation of India was not based on material values or on historical co-existence, but on a moral or religious vocation which goes back to the Upanishads and the Veda. What is most important was education, because only education could get the upper hand over materialism, to which the people of India were exposed.
>
> – Anibel del Campo : "Application of Truth and Non-violence in Gandhi's Teaching and Work", *Truth and Nonviolence,* Gandhi Peace Foundation New Delhi, 1970, pp. 197-198.

When Gandhi speaks of revolutionalisation of education, he wants to correlate education with real life situation. This will as he truly believes, direct education for humanism. While explaining the role of hand-spinning in education at the teachers' training centre at Wardha, he unfolds the immense possibilities of basic education for advancement of humanism :

> Just as a biologist in order to become a good biologist, must learn many other sciences besides biology, the basic education, if it is treated as a science, takes us into the interminable channels of learning. To extend the example of *takli*, a pupil teacher, who rivets his attention not merely on the mechanical process of spinning, which, of course, he must master, but on the spirit of the thing, will concentrate on the *takli* and its various aspects. He will ask him why the *takli* is made out of a brass disc and has a steel spindle. The original *takli* had its disc made anyhow. And the still more primitive *takli* consisted of a wooden spindle with a disc of slate or of clay. The *takli* has been developed scientifically, and there is a reason for making the disc out of brass and the spindle out of steel. He must try to find out the reason. Then the teacher must ask himself why the disc has that particular diameter, no more and no less. When he has solved these questions scientifically and has gone into the mathematics of the thing, your pupil becomes a good engineer. The *takli* becomes his *kamadhenu*, the 'cow of plenty'. There is no limit to the possibilities of knowledge that can be imparted through this medium. It will be limited only by the energy and conviction with which you work.
>
> — D. G. Tendulkar : *Mahatma*, Publications Division, Ministry of Information and Broadcasting, Government of India Vol. V, p. 42.

To make learners 'better men' of the future is what education for humanism really caters to. Gandhi, therefore, urges on the importance of having 'educationists of originality' who might bring about a new dimension of education for rethinking and redesigning human possibilities of making a thrilling adventure in the world of wisdom and erudition, truth and edification. As he observes,

> What we need is educationists with originality fired with true zeal, and who will think out from day-to-day, what they are going to teach their pupils. The teacher can't get this knowledge through the musty volumes. He has to use his own faculties of observation and thinking and impart his knowledge to the children through his lips, with the help of a craft. This means a revolution in the method of teaching, that is, a revolution in the teacher's outlook.
>
> —*Ibid.*

Gandhi further accentuates on revolutionalisation of education :

> Our education has to be revolutionalised. The brain should be educated through the hand. If I were a poet, I could write poetry on the possibilities of five fingers. And why should you think that the mind is everything and the hands and feet are nothing ? Those who don't train the hands, who go through the ordinary rut of education, lack 'music' in their life. All their faculties are not trained. Mere book knowledge does not interest the child, so as to hold attention fully. The brain gets weary of mere words, and the child's mind begins to wander. The hand does the thing it ought not to do, the eye sees the things it ought not to see, and the ear hears the things it ought not to hear, and they do not do, see or hear, respectively, what they ought to. They are not taught to make the right choice and so their education often proves their ruin. An education which does not teach us to discriminate between good and bad, to assimilate the one and eschew the other, is a misnomer.
>
> —*Ibid.*, p. 43.

To make education one's very own to be really of use towards oneself and towards humanity is what education really lacks even today. Gandhi has felt the pulse of the inherent purpose, aims and objectives of education from that basic point of view so that he wants to revolutionalise education as a practical means for the advancement of humanism. To cultivate the mind to think independently in course of discipline is, therefore, an essential objective of education. Let pupils be allowed to exercise their own independent judgements in the pursuit of education. Let them come out of the heaps of books that have already choked their good sense and sensibilities. Let then enjoy the warmth of their own experiences in knowing, feeling and doing. Then and then alone, education becomes living and humanistic. As Gandhi suggests.

> Pupils should know to discriminate between what should be received and what rejected. It is the duty of the teacher to teach his pupils discrimination. If we go on talking indiscriminately we would be no better than machines. We are thinking knowing beings and we must in this period distinguish truth from untruth, sweet from bitter language, clean from unclean things and so on. But the student's path today is strewn with more difficulties than the one of distinguishing good from bad things. The rishis taught their pupils without books. They only gave them a few mantras which the pupils treasured in their memories and translated in practical life. The present day student has to live in the midst of heaps of books, sufficient to choke him.
>
> — M. K. Gandhi : *Young India*, January 29, 1925.

To save pupils from being victims to mere bookish knowledge, Gandhi emphasises on training of the spirit through exercise of inherent humane qualities. The role of the teacher in conducting such spiritual training is undoubtedly very great. It is he who by dint of his balanced life and character sows the seeds of spirituality and humanism in the minds of his pupils. Gandhi's own experience and suggestions in this regard are very significant :

> As I came into closer contact with them (pupils) I saw that it was not through books that one could impart training of the spirit. Just as physical training was to be imparted through physical exercise and intellectual training through intellectual exercise, even so the training of the spirit was possible only through the exercise of the spirit. And the exercise of the spirit entirely depended on the life and character of the teacher. The teacher had always to be mindful of his p's and q's whether he was in the midst of his boys or not.
>
> It is possible for a teacher situated miles away to effect the spirit of the pupils by his way of living. It would be idle for me, if I were a liar, to teach boys to tell the truth. A cowardly teacher

> would never succeed in making his boys valiant, and a stranger to self-restraint could never teach his pupils the value of self-restraint. I saw, therefore, that I must be an eternal object-lesson to the boys and girls living with me. They thus become my teachers, and I learnt I must be good and live straight, if only for their sakes. I may say that the increasing discipline and restraint I imposed on myself at Tolstoy Farm was mostly due to those wards of mine.
>
> — M. K. Gandhi : *An Autobiography*, Navajivan Publishing House, Ahmedabad, 1926, pp. 417-418.

The education of the whole man which is, as Gandhi strongly believes, the education for emancipation of man from his petty little self and for fusion with the Supreme Self is the true education for humanism. Such type of education endears both the intellect and the spirit, physical as well as 'a perfect, well balanced, all-round education'. For 'the education of the heart', Gandhi observes :

> . . . take the case of a child in whom the education of the heart is attended to from the very beginning. Supposing he is set to some useful occupation like spinning, carpentry, agriculture etc., for his education, and in that connection is given a thorough comprehensive knowledge relating to the theory of the various operations that he is to perform, and the use and construction of the tools that he would be wielding. He would not only develop a fine, healthy body but also a sound, vigorous intellect that is not merely academic but is firmly rooted in and is tested from day-to-day experience. His intellectual education would include a knowledge of mathematics and the various sciences that are useful for an intelligent and efficient exercise of his avocation. If to this is added literature by way of recreation, it would give him a perfect, well balanced, all-round education in which the intellect, the body and the spirit have all full play and develop together into a natural, harmonious whole. Man is neither mere intellect, nor the gross animal body, nor the heart or soul alone. A proper and harmonious combination of all the three is required for the making of the whole man and constitutes the true economics of education.
>
> — M. K. Gandhi : *Harijan*, May, 8, 1937.

A synchroniser of humane sensibilities through education of the right mind, right method and right spirit, Gandhi thinks that the drawing out of the best in man necessitates a revolutionary approach where teaching and learning are inter-dependent and the teachers and the learners enjoy freedom of creativity and critical endeavour.

Moreover, for the education of the right mind — the deliverance of man, so to say — Gandhi introduces Basic Education in the truest spirit of efflorescence of religion in developing the human qualities of head and heart. As Shamsuddin remarks,

> Indian culture has all along been influenced by religion in the broadest sense of the term. The sanskrit word *'dharma'* is derived from the root *dhr,* which means to put in or to accept, 'to hold'. Whatever is truth and worth accepting is *dharma,* the rest is *adharma.*
>
> This is the popular meaning of *dharma* or religion according to the *Sastras.* It may be this or that religion, but all religions aim at one common universal aim — a lofty moral and humanitarian outlook.
>
> Gandhi considered religion as an indispensable factor in the system of education. But his opponents sought opportunities for criticising him for the absence of any provision of a religious *book* in the syllabus of Basic Education ! In reply to these critics, Dr. Zakir Hossain once said : "There is no State religion in India. There are followers of various religions and, as such, the teaching of any particular religious book cannot be undertaken here in this land. Moreover, the Gandhian system of basic education provides equal consideration to all religions. It teaches the broad moral principles common to all religions. Truth, non-violence, love for the country, moral uplift and so on are common in all great religions. The Gandhian system of education in fact develops all the good qualities of head and heart in such a way that there is an all-round development of the full personality of the child, making him a patriot in the real sense. In this way, we find a close relationship between basic education and religion".
>
> Shamsuddin : "A few words on Gandhian Education and Religion", *The Visva-Bharati Quarterly,* Gandhi Number, Vol. 35, August 1971, p. 82.

By all-round education Gandhi has a specific viewpoint based on humanism. While opening new schools for imparting such type of education, he writes :

> In the schools I am opening, children under the age of twelve only are admitted. The idea is to get hold of as many children as possible and to give them an all-round education, a good knowledge of Hindi or Urdu and, through that medium, of arithmetic and rudiments of history and geography, a knowledge of simple scientific principles and some industrial training. No cut and dried syllabus has yet been prepared because I am going on an unbeaten track. I look upon our present system with horror and destrust. Instead of developing the moral and mental faculties of the little children it dwarfs them. In my experiment, whilst I shall draw upon what is good in it, I shall endeavour to avoid the defects of the present system. The chief thing aimed at is contact of children with men and women of culture and unimpeachable moral character. That to me is education. Literary training is to be used merely as a means to that end. The industrial training is to be designed for the boys and the girls who may come to us for an additional means of livelihood. It is not intended that on completing their education they should leave their hereditary occupation but make use of the knowledge acquired in the school to refine agriculture and agricultural life. Our teachers will also touch the lives of grown-up people and, if at all possible, penetrate the purdah. Instruction will be given to grown-up people in hygiene and about the advantages of joint action, for the promotion of communal welfare, such as, the making of village roads proper, the sinking of wells, etc. And as no school will be manned by teachers who are not men or women of good training, we propose to give free medical aid as far as possible.
>
> — D. G. Tendulkar : *Mahatma*, Publications Division, Ministry of Information and Broadcasting, Government of India, Vol. I, pp. 211-212.

From the concept of education for advancement of humanism as explained above by Gandhi, it is evident that he always symbolises education as a serene means for inner growth. That inner growth is a challenge eternal. It is the duty of every learner to accept that challenge heroically and march onward from 'Knowledge to more knowledge' dedicated towards the cause of humanism.

Just seven days prior to the independence of India, the words of advice to the students uttered by Gandhi bear the perennial truth of humanism :

> The student's first business is to think out the education that the children of a free nation should receive. The education of today is obviously not such. I must not go into the question as to what it should be. Only they must not allow themselves to be deceived into the belief that it is the function only of the elders in the university senates. They must stimulate the faculty of thinking. I do not even remotely suggest that the students can force the situation by strikes and the like. They have to create the public opinion by offering constructive and enlightened criticism. The senators having been brought up in the old school are slow to move. They can truly be acted upon by enlightenment.
>
> A student's life has been rightly likened to the life of a sanyasi. He must be the embodiment of simple living and high thinking. He must be discipline incarnate. His pleasure is derived from his studies. They do provide the real pleasure when study ceases to be a tax the student has to pay. What can be a greater pleasure than that a student marches from knowledge to more knowledge ?
>
> — D. G. Tendulkar : *Mahatma*, Publications Division, Ministry of Information and Broadcasting, Government of India, Vol. VIII, p. 71.

An apostle of education for radical humanism, Gandhi believes in the beyonding of man.

When comes such another ?

8

TAGORE AND GANDHI : Harbingers of Humanism

> HE STOPPED at the threshold of the huts of the thousands of dispossessed, dressed like one of their own. He spoke to them in their own language. Here was living truth at last, and not only quotation from books. For this reason the Mahatma, the name given to him by the people of India, is his real name, who has felt like him that all Indians are his own flesh and blood ? When love came to the door of India that door was opened wide. At Gandhi's call India blossomed forth to new greatness, just as once before, in earlier times, when the Buddha proclaimed the truth of fellow-feeling and compassion among all living creatures.
>
> — *Rabindranath Tagore*

Great as Gandhi is, greater perhaps than any other humanist of his time in India, Rabindranath Tagore has rightly summed up as above, the whole personality that has totally synchronised with global goodness of mankind. The arduous course for self-preparation to the service of humanity that he has undertaken has perhaps no parallel other than the Christ who was crucified for his dedication and love for mankind. The creative will that Gandhi exercises in course of his pursuit for Truth and Non-violence has proved profoundly effective in transfusing the seeds of humanism among the masses. A creative genius *par excellence*, Rabindranath has to re-evaluate Gandhi in terms of his exceptional creative humanism :

> We who glorify our tendency to ignore reason, installing in its place blind faith, valuing it as spiritual, are ever paying for its cost with the observation of our mind and destiny. I blamed Mahatmaji for exploiting this irrational force of credulity in our people, which might have had a quick result in a superstructure, while sapping the foundation. Thus began my estimate for

Mahatmaji, as the guide of our nation, and it is fortunate for me that it did not end there.

Gandhiji, like all dynamic personalities, needed a vast medium for the proper and harmonious expression of his creative will. This medium he developed for himself, when he assumed the tremendous responsibility of leading the whole country into freedom through countless social ditches and fences and unlimited dullness of barren politics. This endeavour has enriched and mellowed his personality and revealed what was truly significant in his genius. I have since learnt to understand him, as I would understand an artist, not by theories and fantasies of the creed he may profess, but by that expression in his practice which gives evidence to the uniqueness of his mind. In that only true perspective, as I watch him, I am amazed at the effectiveness of his humanity.

— Rabindranath Tagore : "Gandhi The Man", *The Visva-Bharati Quarterly,* Gandhi Number, Visva-Bharati, Santiniketan, 1971, Vol. 35, pp. 30-31.

Disappointment and erosion of humane sensibilities — the two very obstinate negative forces of humanism—did not avert Tagore's inner vision and so he reacts whenever and wherever humanism is in peril. Like Gandhi, he awaits the inner consciousness of every one who promises for poignance of humanism in the exercise of individual freedom for the greatest and best use of creative, aesthetic and humanistic values within himself. As a matter of fact, Tagore, like Gandhi, welcomes all constraints of life heroically as if these are nothing but boosters for the fusion of the All Beautiful and man. The muse that the poet begins is a manifestation of the self in sombre humility and frank confession of ample indebtedness :

Obstinate are the trammels, but my heart aches when I try to break them.

Freedom is all I want, but to hope for it I feel ashamed.

I am certain that priceless wealth is in thee, and that thou art my best friend, but I have not the heart to sweep away the tinsel that fills my room.

The shroud that covers me is a shroud of dust and death; I hate it, yet hug it in love.

My debts large, my failures great, my shame secret and heavy; yet when I come to ask for my good, I quake in fear lest my

> prayer be granted.
>
> — Rabindranath Tagore : *Gitanjali,* Macmillan Pocket Tagore Edition. Macmillan India Limited, New Delhi. 1981, No. 28, pp. 16-17.

An indomitable optimist like Tagore, Gandhi has infinite belief in the endless possibilities of human endeavour. He believes in man's capacity to stick to non-violence under any circumstances. As he observes,

> The more you develop it in your own being, the more infectious it becomes, till it overwhelms your surroundings and by and by might oversweep the world.
>
> — D. G. Tendulkar : *Mahatma,* Publication Division, Ministry of Information and Broadcasting, Government of India, Vol. V, p. 14.

Again, a great believer, like Tagore, in human nature, Gandhi never loses faith in humanity. As he strongly believes,

> The most practical, the most dignified way of going in the world is to take people at their word, when you have no positive reason to the contrary. I refuse to believe that the tendency of the human nature is always downward.
>
> — M. K. Gandhi : *Young India,* December 25, 1926.

In his concept of man, Tagore also heightens humanity, for he also believes that it is a great sin to lose faith in man. Keenly aware of the role of man in a schizophrenic world of ours, he remarks,

> For various unavoidable reasons in the history of man, wars sometimes take place, sometimes, again, peace prevails; the spate of wealth and affluence sometimes occurs or at times its ebb-tide flows. Sometimes man becomes frenzied in his own strength while at times he becomes overwhelmed with the sense of his own helplessness. Under such circumstances, when man is leaning towards one side, it is the true education for him to give a great pull from the other side. When the nature of man remains strong and lively, he selects the harmony of balance by means of an easy force that comes from within his own self. The man who has control over his own body, naturally adjusts himself, when he wants to negotiate a jolt from one end, by balancing on the other side. But an intoxicated person dwindles with a little jolt and

> remains so at that place. The strategies for educating the children in Europe are changing from within. The more their minds are becoming aware of diverse ideas and knowledge through association of experiences, the more are the rapid changes taking place in these avenues.
>
> — Rabindranath Tagore : *Sikshavidhi* (Principles of Education). *Siksha*, Visva-Bharati, 1973, pp. 124-125.
>
> (Translated by the author)

In the Gandhian concept of man, there is the same Tagorean appeal to renew human possibilities with every changeable situation for a balanced adjustment within which will ultimately make fusion between him and the Creator. As Gandhi highlights the human excellence :

> Man and his deed are two distinct things. It is quite proper to resist and attack a system, but to resist and attack its author is tantamount to resisting and attacking oneself. For we are all tarred with the same brush, and are children of the one and the same Creator, and as such the divine powers within us are infinite. To slight a human being is to slight those divine powers, and thus to harm not only that being but with him the whole world.
>
> — M. K. Gandhi : *An Autobiography*, Navajivan Publishing House, Ahmedabad, 1940, p. 337.

Like Tagore, Gandhi also never loses faith in man, He strongly believes that although perfection in life is unattainable, our ceaseless strivings for perfection indicates the fact that we are continually reaching Truth bit by bit. The spirit of non-violence is the spirit of this inherent human nature. As an ordent idealist like Tagore, he thinks :

> The virtue of an ideal consists in its boundlessness. But although religious ideals must thus from their very nature remain unattainable by imperfect human beings, although by virtue of their boundlessness they may seem ever to recede farther and farther away from us, the nearer we go to them, still they are closer to us than our very hands and feet because we are more certain of their reality and truth than even our own physical being. This faith in ideal constitutes real life, in fact, it is man's all in all.
>
> — M. K. Gandhi : *Young India*, November 22, 1928.

Keeping in view the imperfections and broken promises of man, Tagore also endears a deep imperishable faith in the All Beautiful to march on and on with the inner yearnings for better excellence and nobler efflorescence:

> Just as in my heart of hearts
> Your heart does dance
> Let the tornado of your love blow in abundance
> in my heart
> With the shower of juice
> Let it be in unison with all
> Overflowing my offerings
> Let it be our gift.
> My heart remains imprisoned
> within me.
> Take it beside you and deliver it.
> Just as your stars
> Your flowers as well,
> So let it be yours very own
> As your song.
>
> — Rabindranath Tagore : *Geetimalya, Rabindra Rachanavali*, Governmment of West Bengal, Calcutta, 1980. Vol. II, No. 110, p. 359.
>
> (Translated by the author)

The ultimate oneness of man and God as the essence of humanism throws open a new dimension of man who is practically a representative of the inner, purer man within — a spokesman of the All Beautiful. And so the inner vision is reflected in a greater poignance of humanism :

> Thou hast come in lovely apparel in the evening,
> I salute Thee.
> Thou hast smiled in my heart of darkness,
> I salute Thee.
> In this sky humble and silent, beautiful and deep,
> I salute Thee.
> In this air gentle and very calm and dense in drowsiness,
> I salute Thee.
> In this green seat of the tired earth.
> I salute Thee.
> In this silent chanting speech of the dumb stars

I salute Thee.
In this secluded inn at the end of work,
I salute Thee.
In this garland of evening flowers with the feast of fragrance,
I salute Thee.
— Rabindranath Tagore : *Geetimalya*, *Rabindra-Rachanavali*, Government of West Bengal, Calcutta, 1980, Vol. II, No. 112, p. 360.
(Translated by the author)

With the essential belief in oneness of man, Gandhi also advances humanism with the fusion between man and God. This also enhances man's concept of spiritualism, and the world as it should be, becomes more endearing :

> I do not believe that an individual may gain spiritually and those that surround him suffer. I believe in *advaita*, I believe in the essential unity of man and for that matter of all that lives. Therefore, I believe that if one man gains spiritually, the whole world gains with him and if one man fails, the world fails to that extent.
>
> — M.K. Gandhi : *Young India*, December 4, 1924.

Elsewhere

> I believe in absolute oneness of God and therefore also of humanity. What though we have many bodies? We have but one soul. The rays of the sun are many through refraction. But they have the same source.
>
> — M.K. Gandhi : *Young India*, September 25, 1924.

The identity-indifference between man and God, as Gandhi upholds, comes closest to Tagore who also makes a fusion between the two. Gandhi also makes the point more explicit when he remarks :

> Every one of us is a mixture of good and evil. Is there not plenty of evil in us? There is enough in me . . . . and I always pray to God to purge me of it. The difference that there is between human beings is the difference of degree.
>
> — M.K. Gandhi : *Harijan*, June 10, 1939.

Looking upon God as a divergent, dynamic force as Tagore does, Gandhi continually orients his vision of man towards greater humanism :

> Gandhi tries to keep his conception of man and God mobile and dynamic by thinking of God as force, as life etc., as if to make him admit divergent lines of a manifestation, incarnation and inspiration.
>
> — D.M. Dutta : *The Philosophy of Mahatma Gandhi*, The University of Wisconsin Press, Madison, 1953, p. 64.

Perhaps, Tagore's views on Gandhi as a synthesizer of man and for that end in view, as a humanist clarify our idea most prominently :

> An ascetic himself, he does not frown on the joys of others, but works for the enlivening of their existence day and night. He exalts poverty in his own life, but no man in India has striven more assiduously than he for the material welfare of his people. A reformer with the zeal of a revolutionary, he imposes severe restraints on the very passions he provokes. Something of an idolator and also an iconoclast, he leaves the old gods in their dusty niches of sanctity and simply lures the old worship to better and more humane purposes. Professing his adherence to the caste system, he launches his firmest attack against it where it keeps its strongest guards, and yet he has hardly suffered from popular disapprobation as would have been the case with a lesser man who could have much less power to be effective in his efforts.
>
> * * * *
>
> He advises his followers to hate evil without hating the evil-doer. It sounds an impossible precept, but he has made it as true as it can be made in his own life. I had once an occasion to be present at an interview he gave to a certain prominent politician who had been denounced by the official congress party as a deserter. Any other Congress leader would have assumed repelling attitude, but Gandhi was all graciousness and listened to him with patience and sympathy, without once giving him an occasion to feel small. Here, I said to myself, is a truly great man, for he is greater than the party he belongs to, greater even than the creed he professes.
>
> This, then, seems to me to be the significant fact about Gandhiji. Great as he is as a politician, as an organiser, as a leader of men, as a moral reformer, he is greater than all these as a man,

> because none of these aspects and activities limits his humanity. They are rather inspired and sustained by it. Though an incorrigible idealist and given to referring all conduct to certain pet formulae of his own, he is essentially a lover of men and not of mere ideas; which makes him so cautious and conservative in his evolutionary schemes. If he proposes an experiment for society, he must first subject himself to its ordeal. If he calls for a sacrifice, he must first pay its price himself. While many socialists wait for all to be deprived of their privileges before they would part with theirs, this man first renounces before he ventures to make any claims on renunciation of others.
>
> — Rabindranath Tagore : "Gandhi the Man", *The Visva-Bharati Quarterly*, Gandhi Number, Visva-Bharati, Santiniketan, 1971, Vol. 35, pp. 31-32.

Representing himself as a symbol of Truth and purity of the means, Gandhi highlights the glory of man as man. He upholds Truth and Non-violence like a rock and brings forth Goodness and Beauty as the most prized objectives of humanity. Tagore's exposition on Gandhi as a humanist is very telling and poignant :

> His emphasis on the Truth and purity of the means, from which he has evolved his creed of non-violence, is but another aspect of his deep and insistent humanity; for it insists that men in their fight for their claims must only so assert their rights, whether as individuals or as groups, as never to violate their fundamental obligation to humanity, which is to respect life. To say that, because existing rights and privileges of certain classes were originally won and are still maintained by violence, they can only be destroyed by violence, is to create on unending circle of viciousness; for their will always be men with some grievance, fancied or real, against the prevailing order of society, who will claim the same immunity from moral obligation and the right to wade to their goal through slaughter. Somewhere the circle has to be broken, and Gandhiji wants his country to win the glory of first breaking it.
>
> —*Ibid.*, p. 33.

Synchronising work with intellect, the body with the brain, Gandhi shows the avenues of emancipation of man. Tagore also follows the same avenue of experimentation in his own Institute for Rural Development at Sriniketan, Visva-Bharati where he allows the spontaneity of education through work. Gandhi's vision of humanism thus makes a fair ground of fusion in the Tagorean concept of humanism to a great extent:

> He (Gandhi) had great regard for what could be achieved with men's hands and feet. Indeed he used to say, 'There is no point in developing the brain only, one has to develop one's brain through one's hands. If I were a poet, I would write a beautiful poem on the possibilities of the five fingers on one's hand. Those who do not know how to use their hands get little profit out of education. They are like one who sings false notes without feeling the music. Books are never sufficiently interesting to hold the interest of the mind. The mind begins to wander. Only manual work brings you back to reality: Rabindranath Tagore had also taken up this problem. . . .
>
> Today one tends to say that a person is cultured if he does not use his hands. It is necessary to correct this concept of culture and spirituality and recognise and embellish the moral and spiritual qualities of the different occupations of the working classes. And that was for Gandhi completely right. Tagore, himself a poet, spoke highly of the nobility and dignity of the humble tasks of those who worked in his university.
>
> — Anibal del Campo : 'Application of Truth and Non-violence in Gandhi's Teaching and Work', *Truth and Non-violence*, T.K. Mahadevan (Ed.), Gandhi Peace Foundation, New Delhi, 1971, pp. 198-199.

Tagore's education for sympathy and universal brotherhood of mankind that serves as the core of universal humanism appeals to Gandhi for making an earnest endeavour to bring about a social revolution. Tagore's attitude towards greater goodness of a greater society of individuals who continually strive for deeper excellence of humanity is primarily based on finding out and manifesting the excellence of man. That excellence based on individual and social consciousness makes newer avenues of humanism by upholding ancient culture and tradition. While explaining the functions of universities for emancipation of all-embracing goodness of humanity, Tagore remarks :

> There is an aspect of knowledge, which is subjective. It is existent in the greed for collection of materials for knowledge. It excites the pomp of scholarship. No great inspiration finds enthusiasm

towards this store-house of the spendthrift. The reference to the era of the great Indian universities that I had made had meditation within it. This is because it had not the aim to fill in the storehouse. Its objective was to enkindle the universal mind, awakening and creation of character. The ideal of total humanity as reflected in the mind of India in knowledge, action and in ideas of the heart was to be infused through this endeavour in the lives of all for eternity towards economic and other worldly abilities and not towards the intellect alone.

This is also applicable to the institutions of Nalanda and Vikaramsila. In that era, the people of the country intensively understood the invaluable price of learning. There is no doubt that encompassing it in total fulness, the desire to establish a universal seat of knowledge naturally came in the Indian mind.

— Rabindranath Tagore : "*Visvavidyalayer Roop*" *Siksha*, Visva-Bharati, 1973, p. 202.

(Translated by the author)

Tracing the history of human civilisation and social synthesis, Tagore goes deeper into the problems of cultural and social cohesion. As he observes :

The history of man takes different shapes in different countries. The history of India has also its specialities. From the very beginning of her history, we have been visualising that this country is not meant for a particular nation or a particular civilisation. Just as the Aryan civilisation is true in this country, Muslims are not inferior to the Hindus. For this very reason, the very history of this country has, like an enormous meteor, become blurred with the vapour of clashes of diverse conflicts. We have been encountering the commotion of different forces in this history but we have not yet visualised the outcome of an undivided historical image. The distinct cry of an eternally inseparable "I" out of this expanded vastness has not yet ushered forth.

— Rabindranath Tagore : "*Chhatrasasantantra*", *Siksha*, Visva-Bharati, 1973, p. 165.

(Translated by the author)

Tagore's broad spectrum of humanism is further flashed when he welcomes western socio-cultural manners, customs and traditions :

> I am observing that as there are the Aryans, the Dravidians, the Muslims so are also the British. The real history of India is, therefore, not only our history but also the history of the British. Now we will have to see if these different parts of history are properly synchronised and the whole thing becomes a part of the living body. We have no ability to eliminate any of the parts. We could not leave the Muslims aside nor would we be able to leave the English. This is not due to the absence of physical strength, the very nature of the history is this. It is not the history of a particular nation but it is the chemical process of the history of humanity.
>
> — *Ibid.* (Translated by the author)

For such a 'chemical process of the history of humanity' as Tagore foretells, Gandhi steps on with his call for self-sacrifice for emergence of the eternal soul of mankind. A global awakening of humanism awaits mutual sympathy and co-operation that eliminates the baser self and merges in the universal self. As he observes :

> I have but shadowed forth my intense longing to lose myself in the Eternal and become merely a lump of clay in the potter's divine hands so that my service may become more certain . . . .
>
> — M.K. Gandhi : *Young India*, November 17, 1921.

The truth of transcendence of humanism with which both Gandhi and Tagore are baptised is the inner light of awareness of oneness. Tagore terms it as the "indwelling light of oneness" — the light that brings forth the harmony of human consciousness :

> By the indwelling light of this truth, I know that the world to which I belong, and which consists of an endless series of movements, has an inner truth of its own which is one, and which gives reality to the innumerable facts we know about the universe. We realise this inner truth, we experience *Ananda*, Joy, for through Joy we discover the eternal harmony of our own reality.
>
> So often we ignore the real truth of a man and only deal with surface facts about him. The man who sells things to me is, for myself, a mere fact. The man whom I employ as my servant is a bundle of certain facts, all useful in the particular facts and circumstances of my life. Through such facts I find the satisfaction of many of my needs, but no joy. For joy comes only

> when we realise the harmony of the *Satyam*, or Truth, that is in us, with the *Satyam*, or Truth, that is in others, and, in this case, in my servant. But with regard to our loved ones, we are directly aware of the deeper truth which is constantly manifested through them in their outer life, because with them we more easily realise a natural affinity. Their outer activity may hold no value for our own life's purposes, nay it may even be a hindrance. They have, however, an ultimate value for us in that they are, that they embody, an inner truth which is also within me.
>
> — Rabindranath Tagore : "The Philosophical Approach to Sriniketan", L.K. Elmhirst : *Rabindranath Tagore : Pioneer in Education*, Visva-Bharati, 1961, p. 86.

The presence of the 'inner truth' within himself that Gandhi deeply feels is the law of love that embraces all humanity :

> I am impatient to realise the presence of my Maker, who to me embodies Truth and in the early part of my career I discovered that if I was to realise Truth, I must obey, even at the cost of my life, the law of love.
>
> — M.K. Gandhi : *The Nation's Voice*, Navajivan Press, Ahmedabad, 1932, p. 319.

The broader and saner canvas of humanism that Tagore shows in his thoughts for advancement of human endeavour and human sympathy for the universal brotherhood of mankind and translates into reality in his study of 'the mind of man in the realisation of different aspects of truth from diverse points of view' has also its replica of course, with all its diverse dimensions, in Gandhi's thoughts and experiments on humanism. This is evident when he makes the freedom of India wide open to embrace humanism by eliminating hatred and exploitation. As he categorically observes :

> I live for India's freedom and would die, for it, because it is part of Truth. Only a free India can worship the true God. I work for India's freedom because my *swadeshi* teaches me that being born in it and having inherited her culture, I am fittest to serve *her* and *she* has a prior claim to my service. But my patriotism is not exclusive; it is calculated not only not to hurt another nation but to benefit all in the true sense of the word. India's freedom as conceived by me can never be a menace to the world.
>
> — M.K. Gandhi : *Young India*, April 3, 1924.

Elsewhere, he says :

> We want freedom for our country, but not at the expense or exploitation of others, not so as to degrade other countries. I do not want the freedom of India if it means the extinction of England or the disappearance of Englishmen. I want the freedom of my country so that other countries may learn something from my free country, so that the resources of my country might be utilised for the benefit of mankind. Just as the cult of patriotism teaches us today that the individual has to die for the family, the family has to die for the village, the village for the district, the district for the province, and province for the country even so, a country has to be free in order that it may die, if necessary for the benefit of the world. My love therefore of nationalism, or my idea of nationalism, is that my country may become free that if need be, the whole country may die, so that the human races may live. There is no room for race-hatred there.
>
> — Mahadev Desai : *Gandhi in Indian Villages*, G. Ganesan, Triplicane, Madras, 1927, p. 170.

To be in unison with man anywhere and everywhere without making any differences between caste and creed, race and religion etc. is to be in unison with the All Beautiful. While Gandhi reduces himself to a zero to encounter the All Beautiful, Tagore sings on the joy of beholding Him everywhere and within himself in the bright halo of humanism :

My man of my heart is in the heart,
So I behold Him everywhere.
In the stars of eyes, in the stream of light
He exists and so He is not lost.
Ye, so I see Him anywhere and everywhere
Wherever I feast my eyes,
To hear Him speak, I know not where I went
Alas, I heard Him not
Today in my own heart after my return
I hear His message in songs of mine.
Who you are that seek Him like a beggar
from door to door
Never, never will you be able to meet Him.
O, come in a hurry and see in my own breast

In the two eyes of mine.

— Rabindranath Tagore : *Songs, Rabindra-Rachanavali*, Government of West Bengal, Calcutta, 1980, Vol. IV, No. 778.

(Translated by the author)

To discover and re-discover the inner man in the light of freedom, truth and 'human relationship', Tagore makes a new endeavour for education for humanism — an endeavour that emphasises on cultivation of finer sensibilities of life. As he explicitly states :

> I tried to create an atmosphere in my institution, giving it the principal place in our programme of teaching. For atmosphere there must be for developing the sensitiveness of soul, for affording mind its true freedom of sympathy. Apathy and ignorance are the worst forms of bondage for man; they are the invisible walls of confinement that we carry round us when we are in their grip. In educational organisations our reasoning faculties have to be nourished in order to allow our mind its freedom in the words of truth, our imagination for the world of human relationship. This last is even more important than learning the geography of foreign lands.
>
> — Rabindranath Tagore : "A Poet's School", *Rabindranath Tagore: Pioneer in Education* by L.K. Elmhirst, Visva-Bharati, 1961, p. 64.

How to harmonise global human relationship? How to translate humanism into reality: Tagore's answer is Visva-Bharati — 'Where the world makes its home in a single nest' (*Yatra Visvam Bhavatye kanidam*). In spelling out her objective, Tagore says :

> To STUDY THE MIND OF MAN in its realisation of different aspects of truth from diverse points of view.
>
> To bring into more intimate relation with one another through patient study and research, the different cultures of the East on the basis of their underlying unity.
>
> To approach the West from the standpoint of such a unity of the life and thought of Asia.
>
> To seek to realise in a common fellowship of study the meeting of the East and the West, and thus ultimately to strengthen the fundamental condition of world peace through the establishment of free communication of ideas between the two

hemispheres.

And with such ideals in view, to provide at Santiniketan a centre of culture where research into and study of the religion, literature, history, science and art of Hindu, Buddhist, Jain, Islamic, Sikh, Christian, and other civilisations may be pursued along with the culture of the West, with that simplicity in externals which is necessary for true spiritual realisation, in amity, good fellowship and co-operation between the thinkers and scholars of both Eastern and Western countries free from all antagonisms of race, nationality creed or caste and in the name of the One Supreme Being who is *Santam Sivam Advaitam.*

— Rabindranath Tagore : "Aims and Objects", *Santiniketan Vidyalaya* (1901-1961), Visva-Bharati, 1961, p. 3.

That Rabindranath Tagore's message of humanism is the message of eternity can be best understood from a letter by Mahatma Gandhi :

Delhi
1-10-40

Dear Gurudev,

You must stay yet a while. Humanity needs you. I was pleased beyond measure to find that you were better.

With love,
Yours
M.K. Gandhi

— "Letters" *The Visva-Bharati Quarterly*, Gandhi Number, Visva-Bharati, Santiniketan, August 1971, Vol. 35, p. 228.

Are we real followers of Rabindranath Tagore and Mahatma Gandhi, the uncompromising apostles of humanism?

INDEX

Abu Bakr, 59
Advaita, 165
Aesthetic sensibilities, 40
Afflorescence, 104
Agitation, 147
Ahimsa, 19, 20, 22, 37, 45, 46, 70, 71, 92, 100, 111, 113, 124, 131, 135, 143
All Beautiful, 23, 95, 116, 164, 172
Amra Savai raja, 121
Arjuna, 109
Artha, 38
Aryan culture, 61
Ashram, 22
Astronomy, 139
Atman, 114
Atmavat Sarvabhutesu, 75
Automation, 11
Avatars, 93
Barren politics, 161
Basic education, 14, 157
  programmes, 15
Bhagavat-Gita, 36
Bible, 94, 110
Bose, Nirmal Kumar, 29
Brahmacharya, 26, 27, 87, 88, 95
British yoke, 32
Broad-based blue print, 146
Buddha, 160
Carnegies possession, 102
Chakravarti, S., 84
Challenges, 42
Charkha, 13, 17, 133, 134
Christianity, 78
Civil disobedience Gandhi, 119
Compartmentalisation, 141
Constraints, 32
Cow protection, 88
Criticism, 159
Crystallisation, 99
Daridranarayan, 24
Das Gupta, Sujata, 79
Demineering Englishmen, 73
Desai, Mahadev, 34, 64, 65, 149
Dharma, 38, 157
Dharna, 145
Discipline, 120, 122
Divine music, 45
Diwakar, R.R., 58
Domineering Hindus, 73
Dravidians, 170
Durga Das, 89
Dutta, D.M., 166
Education, 69, 74
  humanistic approach of, 137
  objectives of, 138
  programmes of, 148
  revolutionalisation, 153-54
Employment, 140
Exploitation, 29, 66, 72, 83, 84
Freedom. 63
  efflorescence of, 97
Gandhi, M.K., 12, 13, 14, 23, 31, 37, 39, 41, 44, 48, 53, 54, 55, 57, 60, 61, 62, 69, 82, 101, 108, 113, 115, 138, 144, 162, 163
Gandhi's challenge, 111
Gandhian Humanism, 18, 103, 144
  advancement of, 138
  development of, 141
  dissemination of, 143
  efflorescence of, 48, 142
  fundamental aspects of, 16
  global awakening of, 170
  harbingers of, 160
  objectives and strategies of, 25
  poignance of, 164
  socio-cultural aspects of, 59
  starting point of, 12
  strategic policy of, 29, 32
Gandhian non-violence, 126
  philosophy, 86, 151
  viewpoints, 137
General Dyer, 123
Gita, 77, 78, 94, 109
Global awakening, 63
  culture, 127
  socialism, 77
Great Master, 11
Gujarat Vidyapith, 62
Handicrafts, 141, 146
  incorporation of, 149
Harijan, 23, 59, 88, 134
Harmonisation, 51, 127, 130
Harmoy, qualities of, 36
Heart search, 53
Hideous system, 73
Higher education, 139
Hinsa, 20, 22, 38, 92
Human bird, 12
Humanistic education, 141
Incarnation, 166
India's freedom, 171
Industrial training, 158
Industrialisation, 67, 76
Invigorating food, 13
Jalianwala Bagh, 123
Jumma Masjid, 32
Kalpadruma, 117
Kama, 38
Kamadhuk, 140
Karmayogi, 57
Kashi Visvanath temple, 32
Khadi, 88, 110

Kingdom of Heaven, 50
Kisan, 69
Koran, 56
Krishna, 102, 109
Literary training, 158
Mahabharata, 38
Mahadeva, T.M.P., 99
Mammon worship, 76
Manifestation, 36, 161, 166
Marriage, 72
Modern teaching, 143
Moksha, 42
Monatony, 14
Monopolisation, 83
Mother earth, 42
Nalanda, 169
Narayan, J.P., 100
Nayee Talim, 14
New education fellowship programme, 14
Non-co-operation, 117, 122
Non-violence, 18, 20, 77, 106
component of, 136
failure of, 114
principle of, 111
strategies of, 35
Omar, 59
Omnipresence, 47, 81, 82, 94
Panchama 85
Partition of India, 126
Patriotism, 64, 172
Prabhu, R.K., 30, 31, 43, 44, 50, 54, 64, 88, 112, 130, 136
Pradhan, Benudhar, 99
Prem Kirpal, 97, 98
Promote humanism, 151
Purana Swaraj, 76
Pyarelal, 26, 30, 35
Ramachandran, G., 109
Rama Raj, 87
Rao, R.R., 43
Rao, U.R., 30, 31, 44, 50, 64, 130, 136
Rao V.K.R.V., 96
Resolution, 32
Restraints, 26, 78
Revolution, 108, 152
Rishis, 106
Rockefellers, 102
Saiyidani, K.G., 151
Sans, 138
Santam Sivam Advaitam, 174
Sarma, B.S., 100
Sarvodaya, 80, 81, 83, 84, 86, 88, 93, 98, 101, 103, 105
Satyagraha, 71, 78, 106, 115, 117, 118, 124, 132, 133, 135
Satyagrahi, 85, 120, 121
Satyam, 171
Satyanarayana, 80, 81
Self conscience, 48
Self-purification, 19, 43, 46, 48, 65, 75
Self-realisation, 20, 21, 42, 45
Self-restraint, 25, 27, 156
component of, 36
Sevagram Ashram, 110
Sex education, 150
Shamsuddin, 157
Shastras, 49
Shivaji, 59
Shudras, 16, 83
Silent leader, 71
Social disparities, 83
exploitation, 66
Socio-cultural change, 69
disparities, 69
evolution, 70
Socio-astracism, 72
Soul-force, 82, 94, 104
movement, 81
South Africa, 117, 130
Spinning wheel, 15, 16, 68
Spirit of Truth, 19, 45
Srimad Bhagvad Gita, 12
Sri Rama Krishna, 45
Stick-to-itiveness, 13, 17
Strategies, 25
Super-computerisation, 11
Super-divine power 28
Swadeshi, 28, 29, 171
Swami Vivekananda, 28, 45
Swaraj, 13, 17, 75, 85, 86
Synchronisation, 45
Tagore, Rabindranath, 24, 160, 161, 162, 163, 165, 167, 169, 171, 173, 174
education, 168
Takli, 153
Tapas, 49
Tapasya, 48, 49
Teacher's training, 153
Tendulkar, D.G., 16, 18, 22, 33, 36, 39, 55, 60, 68, 71, 117, 126, 127, 150, 153, 158, 159, 162
Tolstoy, 78, 107
farm, 156
Touchstone, 64
Training, 139, 146
Unemployment, 140
Untouchability, 73, 87
Urban exploitation, 148
Utilitarianism, 99
Vasudhaiva Kutumbakam, 30, 48, 82
Vedas, 56
Vikaramsila, 169
Village crafts, 67
Vinoba Bhave, 91
Violence, 92, 114, 119
Visva-Bharati, 167, 173, 174
Wellington, 107
Women education, 143
Yong India, 12, 14, 16, 18, 109
Yoga, 14
Zakir Hussain, 157
Zamindar, 69, 73
Zilliacus, 14